Hands-On Java Deep Learning for Computer Vision

Implement machine learning and neural network methodologies to perform computer vision-related tasks

Klevis Ramo

BIRMINGHAM - MUMBAI

Hands-On Java Deep Learning for Computer Vision

Commissioning Editor: Sunith Shetty
Acquisition Editor: Devika Battike
Content Development Editor: Rhea Henriques
Technical Editor: Dharmendra Yadav
Copy Editor: Safis Editing
Project Coordinator: Manthan Patel
Proofreader: Safis Editing
Indexer: Tejal Daruwale Soni
Graphics: Jisha Chirayil
Production Coordinator: Arvindkumar Gupta

First published: February 2019

Production reference: 1200219

Published by Packt Publishing Ltd.
Livery Place
35 Livery Street
Birmingham
B3 2PB, UK.

ISBN 978-1-78961-396-4

www.packtpub.com

`mapt.io`

Mapt is an online digital library that gives you full access to over 5,000 books and videos, as well as industry leading tools to help you plan your personal development and advance your career. For more information, please visit our website.

Why subscribe?

- Spend less time learning and more time coding with practical eBooks and Videos from over 4,000 industry professionals

- Improve your learning with Skill Plans built especially for you

- Get a free eBook or video every month

- Mapt is fully searchable

- Copy and paste, print, and bookmark content

Packt.com

Did you know that Packt offers eBook versions of every book published, with PDF and ePub files available? You can upgrade to the eBook version at `www.packt.com` and as a print book customer, you are entitled to a discount on the eBook copy. Get in touch with us at `customercare@packtpub.com` for more details.

At `www.packt.com`, you can also read a collection of free technical articles, sign up for a range of free newsletters, and receive exclusive discounts and offers on Packt books and eBooks.

Contributor

About the author

Klevis Ramo is a highly motivated software engineer with a solid educational background who loves writing. He aims to create stable and creative solutions with performance in mind.

Klevis is passionate about coding and machine learning with several open source contributions and is experienced at developing web services and REST API. He is always eager to learn new technologies and to improve system performance and scalability.

Packt is searching for authors like you

If you're interested in becoming an author for Packt, please visit `authors.packtpub.com` and apply today. We have worked with thousands of developers and tech professionals, just like you, to help them share their insight with the global tech community. You can make a general application, apply for a specific hot topic that we are recruiting an author for, or submit your own idea.

Table of Contents

Preface

The aim of this book is to walk you through the process of efficiently training deep neural networks for computer vision using the most modern techniques. The course is designed to get you familiar with deep neural networks in order to be able to train them efficiently, customize existing state-of-the-art architectures, build real-world Java applications, and achieve great results in a short space of time. You will build real-world computer vision applications, ranging from simple Java handwritten digit recognition to real-time Java autonomous car driving systems and face recognition.

By the end of the book, you will have mastered the best practices and most modern techniques to facilitate the building of advanced computer vision Java applications and achieve production-grade accuracy.

Who this book is for

This book is intended for data scientists, machine learning developers, and deep learning practitioners with a knowledge of Java who want to implement machine learning and deep neural networks in the computer vision domain. A basic knowledge of Java programming will be required.

What this book covers

Chapter 1, *Introduction to Computer Vision and Training Neural Networks*, introduces the reader to the concepts of deep neural networks and their learning process. We shall also learn how to train a neural network model in the most efficient manner.

Chapter 2, *Convolution Neural Network Architectures*, explains how a convolutional network is a fundamental part of computer vision and describes how to build a handwritten digit recognizer.

Chapter 3, *Transfer Learning and Deep CNN Architectures*, delves into the details of widely used deep convolution architectures and how to use transfer learning to get the most out of these architectures. This chapter concludes with the building of a Java application for animal image classification

Chapter 4, *Real-Time Object Detection*, covers how to additionally mark objects with boundary boxes in real time. We will use these techniques and ideas to build a Java real-time car pedestrian and traffic light detection system that is the basis for autonomous driving.

Chapter 5, *Creating Art with Neural Style Transfer*, explains how we want to know what deep neural network layers are trying to learn. We will use this intuition and knowledge to build a new lifestyle transfer application in Java that is able to create art.

Chapter 6, *Face Recognition*, helps the reader to solve the problem of face recognition and ultimately compile a Java face recognition application.

To get the most out of this book

This book will teach you how to build advanced machine learning applications with intuitive and detailed explanations of topics, and with no background in math required. It adopts a practical approach by applying the theory to build real-world Java applications using modern practices and techniques that are prevalent in the computer vision world.

Download the example code files

You can download the example code files for this book from your account at www.packt.com. If you purchased this book elsewhere, you can visit www.packt.com/support and register to have the files emailed directly to you.

You can download the code files by following these steps:

1. Log in or register at www.packt.com.
2. Select the **SUPPORT** tab.
3. Click on **Code Downloads & Errata**.
4. Enter the name of the book in the **Search** box and follow the onscreen instructions.

Once the file is downloaded, please make sure that you unzip or extract the folder using the latest version of:

- WinRAR/7-Zip for Windows
- Zipeg/iZip/UnRarX for Mac
- 7-Zip/PeaZip for Linux

The code bundle for the book is also hosted on GitHub at `https://github.com/PacktPublishing/Hands-On-Java-Machine-Learning-for-Computer-Vision`. In case there's an update to the code, it will be updated on the existing GitHub repository.

We also have other code bundles from our rich catalog of books and videos available at `https://github.com/PacktPublishing/`. Check them out!

Download the color images

We also provide a PDF file that has color images of the screenshots/diagrams used in this book. You can download it here: `https://www.packtpub.com/sites/default/files/downloads/9781789613964_ColorImages.pdf`.

Conventions used

There are a number of text conventions used throughout this book.

`CodeInText`: Indicates code words in text, database table names, folder names, filenames, file extensions, pathnames, dummy URLs, user input, and Twitter handles. Here is an example: "Now, `detectEdges` is exposed to the graphical user interface, to detect edges, and it takes two inputs: the colored image, `bufferedImage`, and the filter selected by the user, `selectedFilter`."

A block of code is set as follows:

```
package ramo.klevis.ml;
import javax.imageio.ImageIO;
import java.awt.*;
import java.awt.image.BufferedImage;
import java.io.File;
import java.io.IOException;
import java.util.HashMap;
public class EdgeDetection {
```

Bold: Indicates a new term, an important word, or words that you see on screen. For example, words in menus or dialog boxes appear in the text like this. Here is an example: "So if we take the block highlighted in the screenshot, we'll multiply **1** by **255**, add **0** multiplied by **255**, and then subtract **1** multiplied by **255**."

 Warnings or important notes appear like this.

 Tips and tricks appear like this.

Get in touch

Feedback from our readers is always welcome.

General feedback: If you have questions about any aspect of this book, mention the book title in the subject of your message and email us at customercare@packtpub.com.

Errata: Although we have taken every care to ensure the accuracy of our content, mistakes do happen. If you have found a mistake in this book, we would be grateful if you would report this to us. Please visit www.packt.com/submit-errata, selecting your book, clicking on the Errata Submission Form link, and entering the details.

Piracy: If you come across any illegal copies of our works in any form on the internet, we would be grateful if you would provide us with the location address or website name. Please contact us at copyright@packt.com with a link to the material.

If you are interested in becoming an author: If there is a topic that you have expertise in, and you are interested in either writing or contributing to a book, please visit authors.packtpub.com.

Reviews

Please leave a review. Once you have read and used this book, why not leave a review on the site that you purchased it from? Potential readers can then see and use your unbiased opinion to make purchase decisions, we at Packt can understand what you think about our products, and our authors can see your feedback on their book. Thank you!

For more information about Packt, please visit `packt.com`.

Introduction to Computer Vision and Training Neural Networks

1

In this chapter, we will introduce the topic of computer vision and focus on the computer vision state and its applications. By learning to train neural networks with the help of deep learning, we will understand the parallels between the human brain and a neural network by representing the network in a computer system. To optimize our training results, we will also look at effective training techniques and optimization algorithms, which will dramatically decrease the neural network training time, enabling us to have deeper neural networks trained with more data. We will put all of these optimization techniques or parameters together and give a systematic process for accurately choosing their values.

Additionally, we will learn to organize data and the application that we will be creating. At the end of this chapter, we will take a closer look at how a computer perceives vision and images and how to enable a neural network to actually predict many classes.

The chapter will cover the following topics:

- The computer vision state
- Exploring neural networks
- The learning methodology of neural networks
- Organizing data and applications
- Effective training techniques
- Optimizing algorithms
- Configuring the training parameters of the neural network
- Representing images and outputs
- Building a handwritten digit recognizer

The computer vision state

In this section, we will look at how computer vision has grown over the past couple of years into the current field of computer vision we have today. As mentioned before, the progress in the field of deep learning is what propelled computer vision to advance.

Deep learning has enabled a lot of applications that seemed impossible before. These include the following:

- **Autonomous driving**: An algorithm is able to detect the location of pedestrians and other cars, helping to make decisions about the direction of the vehicle and avoid accidents.
- **Face recognition and smarter mobile applications**: You may already have seen phones that can be unlocked using facial recognition. In the near future, we could have security systems based on this; for example, the door of your house may be unlocked by your face or your car may start after recognizing your face. Smart mobile applications with fancy features such as applying filters and grouping faces together have also improved drastically.
- **Art generation**: Even generating art will be possible, as we will see during this book, using computer vision techniques.

What is really exciting is that we can use some of these ideas and architectures to build applications.

The importance of data in deep learning algorithms

The main source of knowledge for deep learning algorithms is data. Therefore, the quality and the amount of data greatly affects the performance of every algorithm.

For speech recognition, we have a decent amount of data, considering the complexity of the problem. Although the dataset for the images has dramatically improved, having a few more samples will help achieve better results for image recognition. On the other hand, when it comes to object detection, we have less data due to the complexity in the effort of marking each of the objects with a bounding box as shown in the diagram.

Computer vision is, in itself, a really complex problem to solve. Imagine having a bunch of pixels with decimal values, and from there, you have to figure out what they represent.

For this reason, computer vision has developed more complex techniques, larger and more complex architectures, and also a lot of parameters to tune. The rule is such that the less data you have, the more hacks are needed, the more engineering or manual creation of features is required, and the architectures tend to grow complex. On the other hand, if you have more data, the deep learning algorithm tends to do well, and hand-engineering the data becomes a whole lot easier, which means we don't have to tune the parameters and the network architectures stay simple.

Throughout this book, we'll look at several methods to tackle computer vision challenges, such as transfer learning using well-known architectures in literature and opera. We will also make good use of open source implementations. In the next section, we'll start to understand the basics of neural networks and their representations.

Exploring neural networks

In this section, we will learn how artificial neural networks and neurons are connected together. We will build a neural network and get familiar with its computational representation.

Neural networks were first inspired by biological neurons. When we try to analyze the similarities between an artificial network and a neuron, we realize there isn't much in common. The harsh truth here is that we don't even know what a single neuron does and there are still knowledge gaps regarding how connected neurons learn together so efficiently. But if we were to draw conclusions, we could say that all neurons have the same basic structure, which consists of two major regions:

- The region for receiving and processing incoming information from other cells. This involves the dendrites, which receives the input information, and the nucleus, which processes or transforms the information.
- The region that conducts and transmits information to other cells. The axon, or the axon terminals, forward this information to many other cells or neurons.

Building a single neuron

Let's understand how to implement a neural network on a computer by expressing a single neuron mathematically, as follows:

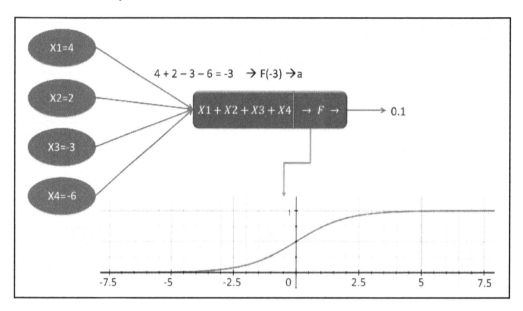

The inputs here are numbers, followed by the computational units. We are familiar with the fact that we do not know the functioning of a biological neuron, but while creating an artificial network, we actually possess the power to build a process.

Let us build a computational unit that will process the data in two steps as depicted in the previous diagram. The first step will sum all the input values obtained so far, and for the second step, we will apply the sum attained in the previous step to a sigmoid function as depicted in the preceding diagram.

The purpose of the sigmoid function is to provide the output as 1 when the sum applied is positive, and to give the output as 0 when the sum applied is negative. In this example, the sum of X1, X2, X3, and X4 will be -3, which, when applied to the sigmoid function, will give us the final value of 0.1.

The sigmoid function, which is applied after the sum, is called the activation function, and is denoted by *a*.

Building a single neuron with multiple outputs

As stated previously, a biological neuron provides the outputs to multiple cells. If we continue to use the example in the previous section, our neuron should forward the attained value of 0.1 to multiple cells. For this sake of this situation, let's assume that there are three neurons.

If we provide the same output of 0.1 to all the neurons, they will all give us the same output, which isn't really useful. The question that now begs an answer is why we need to provide this to three or multiple neurons, when we could do it with only one?

To make this computationally useful, we apply some weights, where each weight will have a different value. We multiply the activation function with these weights to gain different values for each neuron. Look at the example depicted in the following diagram:

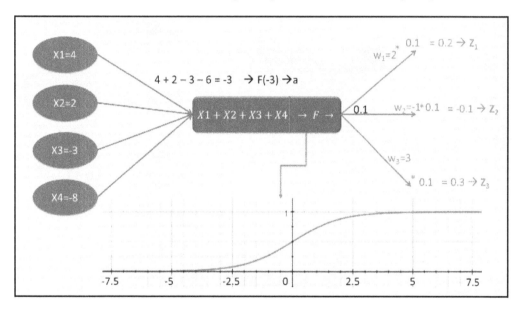

Here, we can clearly see that we assign the values $w_1=2$, $w_2=-1$, and $w_3=3$ to the three weights and obtain the outputs $z_1=0.2$, $z_2=-0.1$, and $z_3=0.3$. We can actually connect these different values to three neurons and the output achieved will be different.

Building a neural network

So now that we have the structure for one neuron, it's time to build a neural network. A neural network, just like a neuron, has three parts:

- The input layer
- The output layer
- The hidden layers

The following diagram should help you visualize the structure better:

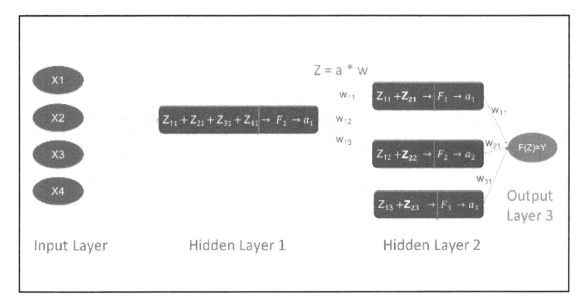

Usually, we have many hidden layers with hundreds and thousands of functions, but here, we have just two hidden layers: one with one neuron and the second with three neurons.

The first layer will give us one output that is achieved after multiplying by the activation function. By applying different values of weights to this, we can produce three different output values and connect them to three new rows, each of which will be multiplied by an activation function. Lastly, sum up these values and apply it to a sigmoid function to obtain the final output. You could add more hidden layers to this as well.

The indexes assigned to each weight in the diagram are decided based on the starting neuron of the first hidden layer and the neuron of the second hidden layer. Thus, the indexes for the weights in the first first hidden later are w_{11}, w_{12}, and w_{13}.

The indexes for the Z value are also assigned in a similar manner. The first index represents the neuron that requires the weight, and the second index of Z represents the hidden layer that the Z value belongs to.

Similarly, we may want the input layer to be connected to different neurons, and we can do that simply by multiplying the input values by weights. The following diagram depicts an additional neuron in hidden layer 1:

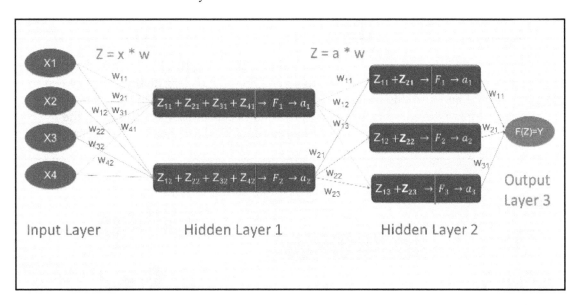

Notice how now we added a bunch of other Zs, which are simply the contribution of this neuron. The second index for this will be 2, because it comes from the second neuron.

The last thing in this section is trying to make a clear distinction between the weights and the Z values that have the same indexes, but actually belong to different hidden layers. We can apply a superscript, as shown in the following diagram:

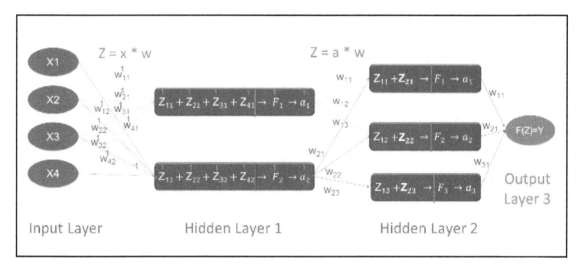

This implies that all the weights and Z values are contributing to a heightened level 1. To further distinguish, we can have 2 added to layer 2, making a clear distinction between the weight in layer 1 and and this weight in layer 2. These contribute to the heightened layer 2, and we can add 3 to the weights for the output layer because those contribute to the heightened output layer 3. The following diagram depicts all the heightened layers:

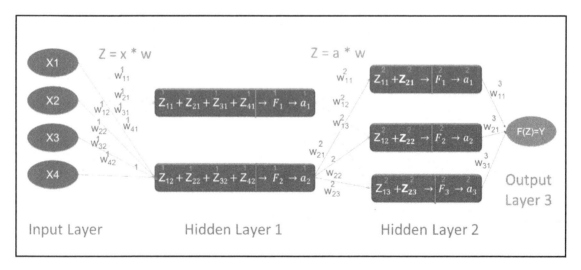

In general, we will mention the superscript index only if it is necessary, because it makes the network messy.

How does a neural network learn?

In this section, we will understand how a simple model predicts and how it learns from data. We will then move on to deep networks, which will give us some insight on why they are better and more efficient compared to other networks.

Assume we are given a task to predict whether a person could have heart disease in the near future. We have a considerable amount of data about the history of the individual and whether they got heart disease later on or not.

The parameters that will be taken into consideration are age, height, weight, genetic factors, whether the patient is a smoker or not, and their lifestyle. Let us begin by building a simple model:

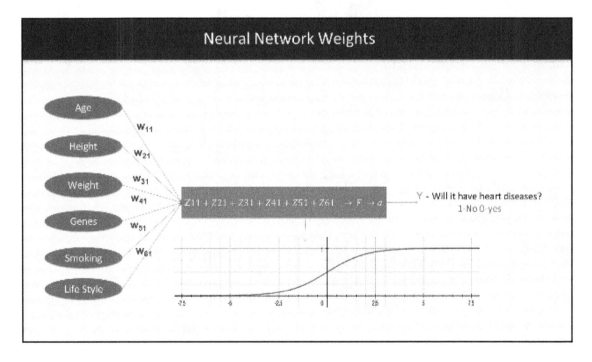

All the information we have for the individual we will use as input, and call them features. As we learned in the previous section, our next step is to multiply the features by the weights, and then take the sum of these products and apply it as an input to a sigmoid function, or the activation function. The sigmoid function will output 1 or 0, depending on whether the sum is positive or negative:

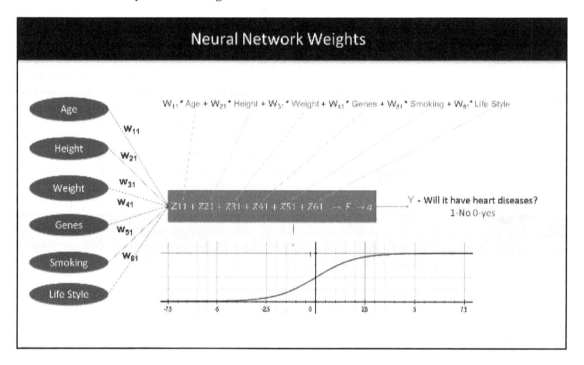

In this case, the activation value produced by the activation function is also the output, since we don't have any hidden layers. We interpret the output value 1 to mean that the person will not have any heart disease, and 0 as the person will have heart disease in the near future.

Let's use a comparative example with three individuals to check whether this model functions appropriately:

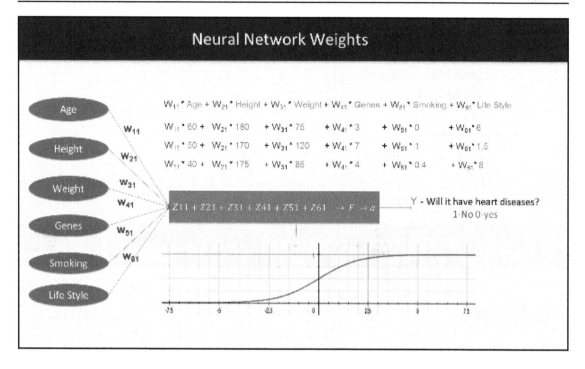

As we can see in the preceding diagram, here are the input values for person 1:

- Age = 60 years old
- Height = 180 centimeters
- Weight = 75 kilograms
- Number of people in their family affected by a heart disease = 3
- Non-smoker
- Has a good lifestyle

The input values for person 2 are as follows:

- Age = 50 years old
- Height = 170 centimeters
- Weight = 120 kilograms
- Number of people in their family affected by a heart disease = 7
- Smoker
- Has a sedentary lifestyle

The input values for person 3 are as follows:

- Age = 40 years old
- Height = 175 centimeters
- Weight = 85 kilograms
- Number of people in their family affected by a heart disease = 4
- Light smoker
- Has a very good and clean lifestyle

So if we had to come up with some probability for each of them having a heart disease, then we may come up with something like this:

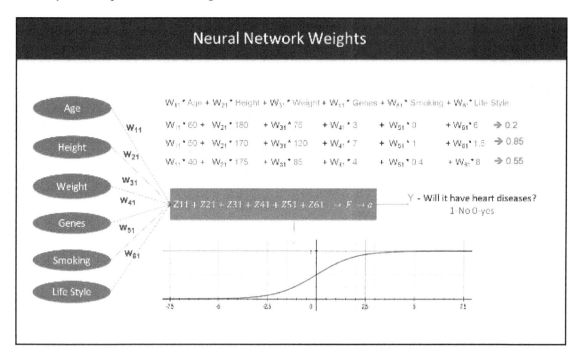

So, for person 1, there is just a 20% chance of heart disease because of his good family history and the fact that they're not smoking and has a good lifestyle. For person 2, it's obvious that the chances of being affected by heart disease are much higher because of their family history, heavy smoking, and their really bad lifestyle. For person 3, we are not quite sure, which is why we give it a 50/50; since the person may smoke slightly, but also has a really good lifestyle, and their family history is not that bad. We also factor in that this individual is quite young.

So if we were to ponder about how we as humans learned to predict this probability, we'd figure out the impact of each of the features on the person's overall health. Lifestyle has a positive impact on the overall output, while genetics and family history have a very negative impact, weight has a negative impact, and so on.

It just so happens that neural networks also learn in a similar manner, the only difference being that they predict the outcome by figuring out the weights. When it comes to lifestyle, a neural network having a large weight for lifestyle will help reinforce the positive value of lifestyle in the equation. For genetics and family history, however, the neural network will assign a much smaller or negative value to contribute the negative factor to the equation. In reality, neural networks are busy figuring out a lot of weights.

Now let's see how neural networks actually learn the weights.

Learning neural network weights

To understand this section, let us assume that the person in question will eventually and indefinitely be affected by a heart disease, which directly implies that the output of our sigmoid function is 0.

We begin by assigning some random non-zero values to the weights in the equation, as shown in the following diagram:

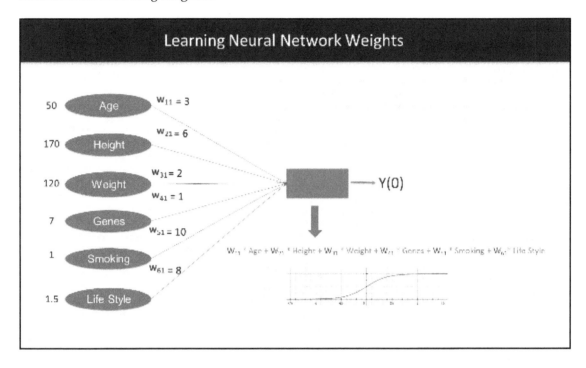

We do this because we do not really know what the initial value of the weights should be.

We now do what we have learned in the previous section: we move in the forward direction of our network, which is from the input layer to the output layer. We multiply the features with the weights and sum them up before applying them to the sigmoid function. Here is what we obtain as the final output:

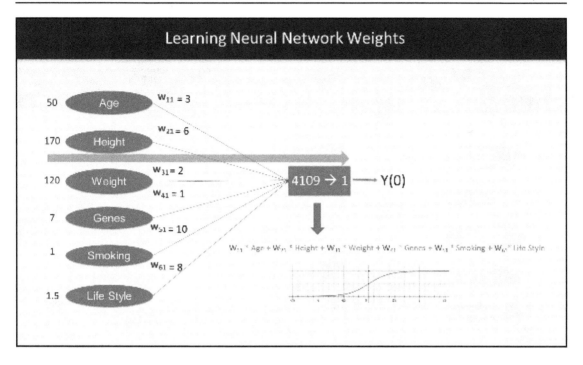

The output obtained is 4109, which, when applied to the activation function, gives us the final output of 1, which is the complete opposite of the actual answer that we were looking for.

What do we do to improve the situation? The answer to this question is a backward pass, which means we move through our model from the output layer to the input layer so that during the next forward pass, we can obtain much better results.

To counter this, the neural network will try to vary the values of the weights, as depicted in the following diagram:

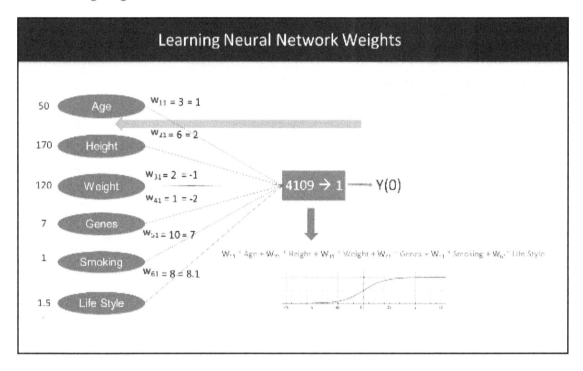

It lowers the weight of the age parameter just to make the age add negatively to the equation. Also, it slightly increases the lifestyle because this contributes positively, and for the genes and weights, it applies negative weights.

We do another forward pass, and this time we have a smaller value of 275, but we're still going to achieve an output one from the sigmoid function:

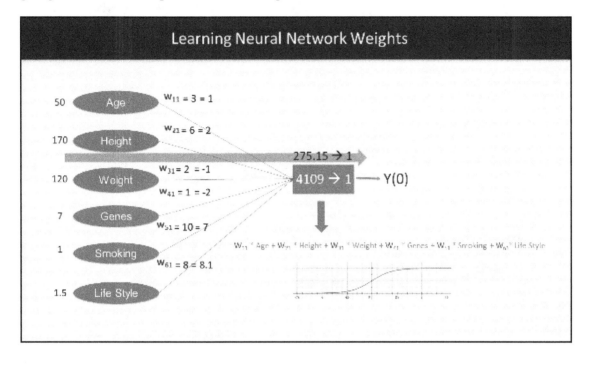

We do a backward pass again and this time we may have to vary the weights even further:

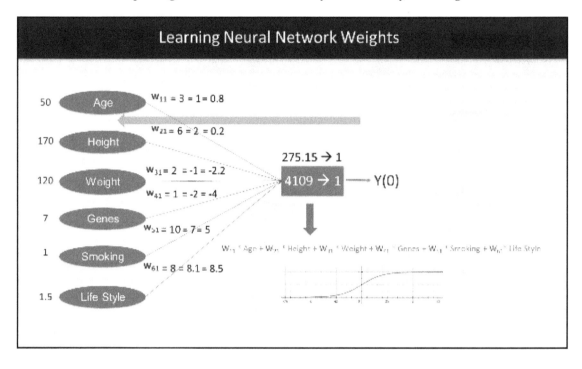

The next time we do a forward pass, the equation produces a negative value, and if we apply this to a sigmoid function, we have a final output of zero:

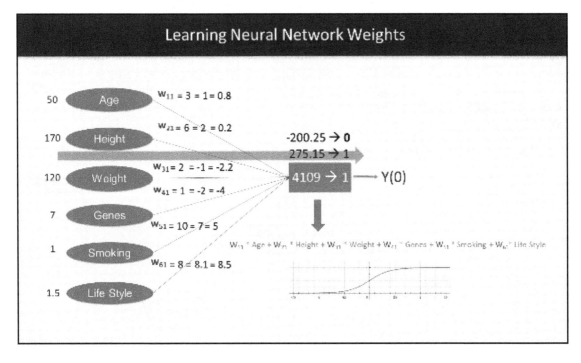

Comparing 0 to the required value, we realize it's time to stop because the network now knows how to predict.

A forward pass and a backward pass together is called one iteration. In reality, we have 1,000, 100,000, or even millions of these examples, and before we change the weight, we take into account the contribution of each of these examples. Basically, we sum up the contribution of each of these examples, and then change the weights.

Updating the neural network weights

The sum of the product of the features and weights is given to the sigmoid or activation function. This is called the hypothesis. We begin with theories on what the output will look like, and then see how wrong we are when the results turn out to be different to what we actually require.

To realize how inaccurate our theories are, we require a loss, or cost, function:

$$J = 1/m * sum(H(w) - Y)^2 - Loss Function$$

The loss or cost function is the difference between the hypothesis and the real value that we know from the data. We need to add the sum function to make sure that the model accounts for all the examples and not only *1*. The reason we square the value is so that we can maintain a positive value and exaggerate the difference between the true data and the error, such that the neural network will work harder to maintain as low an error rate as possible.

The plot for the cost function is as follows:

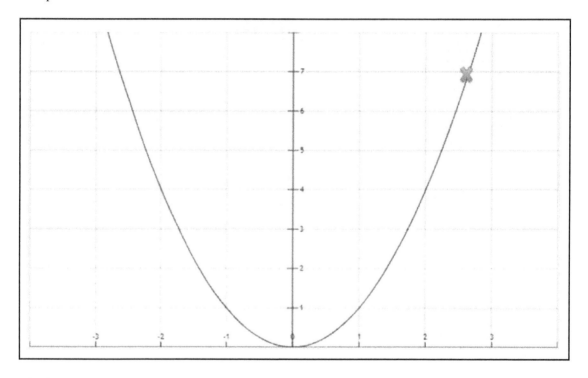

The first hypothesis is marked on the plot. We want the hypothesis that produces a cost value at the zero point because we want the hypothesis to be equal to reality, and they are equal, as we can see from the previous equation. This means that the difference is zero. But, as we saw at the beginning, we start really far away from this value.

Now we need to act on the cost function value to check the accuracy and performance of the hypothesis. In order to understand the direction in which we need to move, we need to calculate the derivative of the cost function by each of the weights. Graphically, that is interpreted as the plot on the following graph, which is tagged with the current cost value:

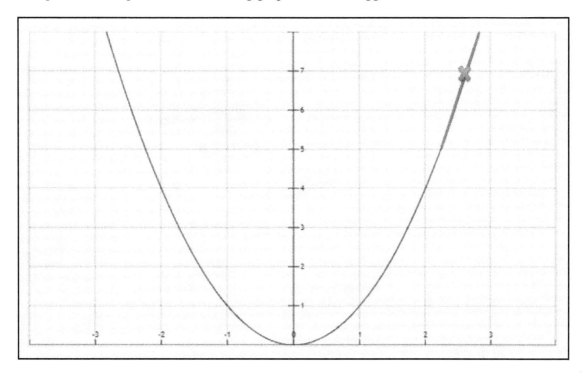

We subtract the derivation value from the actual weights. This is mathematically given as follows:

$$W11 = W11 - \alpha \frac{dJ}{dW_{11}},$$

$$W21 = W21 - \alpha \frac{dJ}{dW_{21}},$$

$$W31 = W31 - \alpha \frac{dJ}{dW_{31}},$$

And so on...

We keep subtracting these values, iteration by iteration, just doing forward and backward passes, and keep moving closer to the zero point:

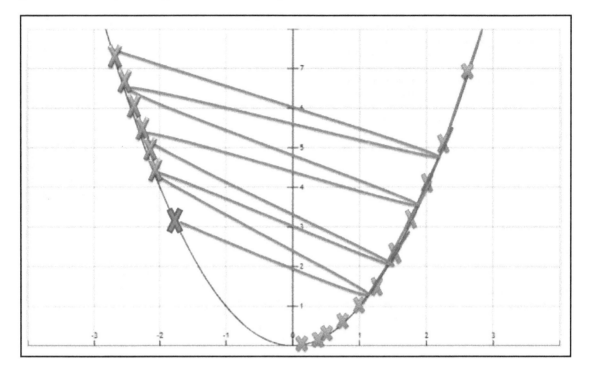

Notice the alpha here, or the learning rate. The learning rate actually defines how big the step is. If we have smaller values then the step is really small and it takes longer to get the desired value, which slows down the neural network learning, while having bigger values may actually cause our model to never get to the desired point. The alpha learning rate has to be just right.

As a sanity check, we can monitor the cost function so that it will increase iteration by iteration, and it should decrease in the long term.

Advantages of deep learning

If we consider a simple model, here is what our network would look as follows:

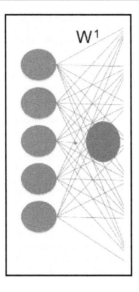

This just means that a simple model learns in one big step. This may work fine for simple tasks, but for a highly complex tasks such as computer vision or image recognition, this is not enough. Complex tasks require a lot of manual engineering to achieve good precision. To do this, we add a lot of other layers of neurons that enable the network to learn step by step, instead of taking one huge leap to the output. The network should look as follows:

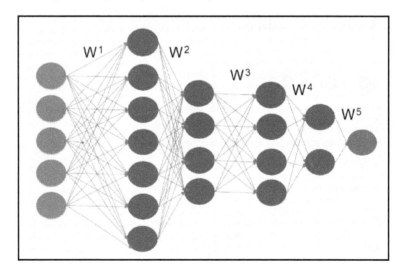

The first layer may learn low-level features such as horizontal lines, vertical lines, or diagonal lines, then it passes this knowledge to the second layer, which learns to detect shapes, then the third layer learns color and shapes, and detects more complex things such as faces and so on. By the fourth and the fifth layer, we may be able to detect really high-level features such as humans, cars, trees, or animals.

Another advantage of deep networks is to picture the output as the function of the input. In a simple model, we have the output that is the indirect function of the input. Here, we can see the output actually is the function of the fifth-layer weights. Then the fifth-layer weights are a function of the fourth layer, and the fourth layer is a function of the third layer, and so on. In this way, we actually learn really highly complex functions compared to a simple model.

So that's it for this section. The next section will be about organizing your data and applications, and at the same time, we will look at a highly efficient computational model for neural networks.

Organizing data and applications

In this section, we will look at the old and new techniques for organizing data. We will also gain some intuition as to what results our model may produce until it is ready for production. By the end of this section, we will have explored how neural networks are implemented to obtain a really high performance rate.

Organizing your data

Just like any other network, a neural network depends on data. Previously, we used datasets containing 1,000 to 100,000 rows of data. Even in cases where more data was added, the low computational power of the systems would not allow us to organize this kind of data efficiently.

We always begin with training our network, which implies that we in fact need a training dataset that should consist of 60% of the total data in the dataset. This is a very important step, as here is where the neural network learns the values of the weights present in the dataset. The second phase is to see how well the network does with data that it has never seen before, which consists of 20% of the data in the dataset. This dataset is known as a `cross-validation` dataset. The aim of this phase is to see how the the network generalizes data that it was not trained for.

Based on the performance in this phase, we can vary the parameters to attain the best possible output. This phase will continue until we have achieved optimum performance. The remaining data in the dataset can now be used as the test dataset. The reason for having this dataset is to have a completely unbiased evaluation of the network. This is basically to understand the behavior of the network toward data that it has not seen before and not been optimized for.

If we were to have a visual representation of the organization of data as described previously, here is what it would look like as in the following diagram:

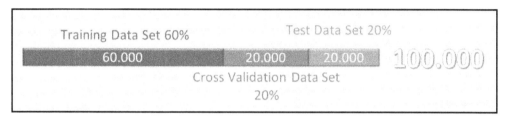

This configuration was well known and widely used until recent years. Multiple variations to the percentages of data allocated to each dataset also existed. In the more recent era of deep learning, two things have changed substantially:

- Millions of rows of data are present in the datasets that we are currently using.
- The computational power of our processing systems has increased drastically because of advanced GPUs.

Due to these reasons, neural networks now have a deeper, bigger, and more complex architecture. Here is how our data will be organized:

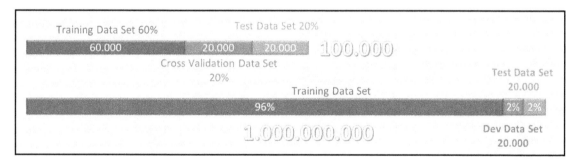

The training dataset has increased immensely; observe that 96% of the data will be used as a dataset, while 2% will be required for the development dataset and the remaining 2% for the testing dataset. In fact, it is even possible to have 99% of the data used to train the model and the remaining 1% of data to be divided between the training and the development datasets. At some points, it's OK to not have a test dataset at all. The only time we need to have a test dataset is when we need to have a completely unbiased evaluation. Through the course of this chapter, we shall hardly use the test dataset.

Notice how the `cross-validation` dataset becomes the development dataset. The functionality of the dataset does not vary.

Bias and variance

During the training of the neural network, the model may undergo various symptoms. One of them is high bias value. This leads to a high error rate on our training dataset and therefore, consecutively, a similar error on the development dataset. What this tells us is that our network has not learned how to solve the problem or to find the pattern. Graphically, we can represent the model like this:

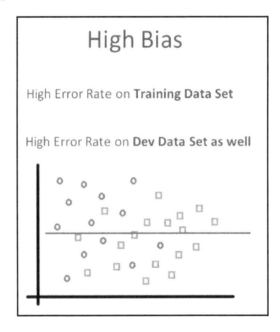

This graph depicts senior boundaries and the errors caused by the model, where it marks the red dots as green squares and vice versa.

We may also have to worry about the high variance problem. Assume that the neural network does a great job during the training phase and figures out a really complex decision bundle, almost perfectly. But, when the same model uses the development testing dataset, it performs poorly, having a high error rate and an output that is not different from the high bias error graph:

If we look at the previous graph, it looks like a neural network really learned to be specific to the training dataset, and when it encounters examples it hasn't seen before, it doesn't know how to categorize our data.

The final unfortunate case is where our neural network may have both of these two symptoms together. This is a case where we see a high error rate on the training dataset and a double or higher error rate for the development dataset. This can be depicted graphically as follows:

The first line is the decision boundary from the training dataset, and the second line is the decision boundary for the development dataset, which is even worse.

Computational model efficiency

Neural networks are currently learning millions of weights. Millions of weights mean millions of multiplications. This makes it essential to find a highly efficient model to do this multiplication, and that is done by using matrices. The following diagram depicts how weights are placed in a matrix:

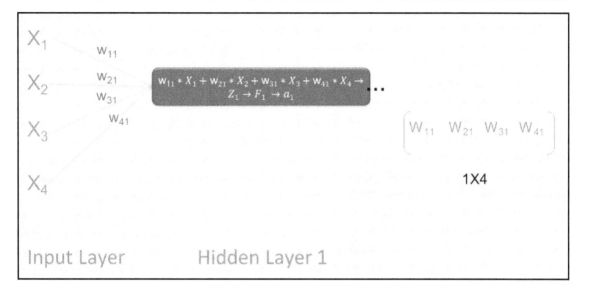

The weight matrix here has one row and four columns, and the inputs are in another matrix. These inputs can be the outputs of the previous hidden layer.

To find the output, we need to simply perform a simple multiplication of these two matrices. This means that Z_1 is the multiplication of the row and the column.

To make it more complex, let us vary our neural network to have one more hidden layer.

Having a new hidden layer will change our matrix as well. All the weights from the hidden layer 2 will be added as a second row to the matrix. The Z_2 value is the multiplication of the second row of the matrix with the column containing the input values:

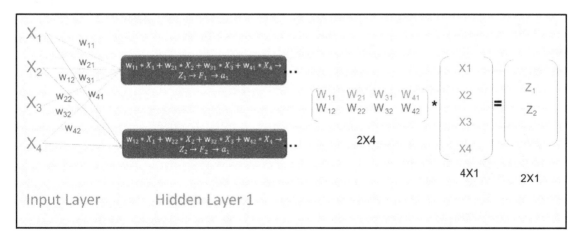

Notice now how Z_1 and Z_2 can be actually calculated in parallel, because they don't have any dependents, so really, the multiplication of the first row with the inputs column is not dependent on the multiplication of the second row with the inputs column.

To make this more complex, we can have another set of examples that will affect the matrix as follows:

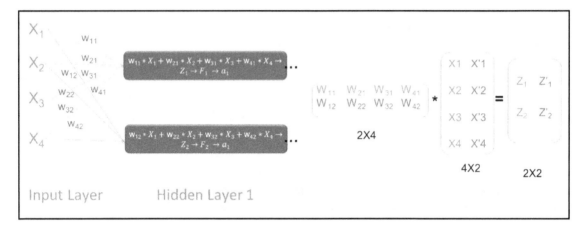

We now have four sets and we can actually calculate each of them in parallel. Consider Z_1, which is the result of the multiplication of the first row with the first input column, while this Z_2' is the multiplication of the second row of weights with the second column of the input.

In standard computers, we currently have 16 of these operations carried out in parallel. But the biggest gain here is when we use GPUs, because GPUs enable us to execute from 100 to 1,000 of these operations in parallel. One of the reasons that deep learning has been taking off recently is because of GPUs offering really great computational power.

Effective training techniques

In this section, we will explore several techniques that help us to train the neural network quickly. We will look at techniques such as preprocessing the data to have a similar scale, to randomly initializing the weights to avoid exploding or vanishing gradients, and more effective activation functions besides the sigmoid function.

We begin with the normalization of the data and then we'll gain some intuition on how it works. Suppose we have two features, X1 and X2, taking a different range of values—X1 from 2 to 5, and X2 from 1 to 2—which is depicted in the following diagram:

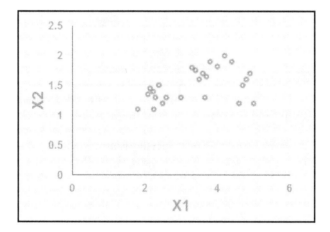

We will begin by calculating the mean for each of the features using the following formula:

$$\mu_1 = avg(X_1), \mu_2 = avg(X_2)$$

After that, we'll subtract the mean from the appropriate features using the following formula:

$$X_1' = X_1 - \mu_1, X_2' = X_2 - \mu_2$$

The output attained will be as follows:

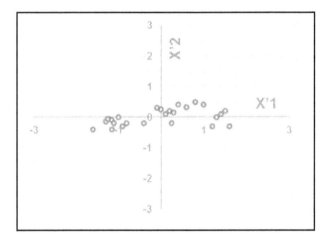

Features that have a similar value to the mean will be centered around the 0, and those having different values will be far away from the mean.

The problem that still persists is the variant. X'_1 has greater variance than X'_2 now. In order to solve the problem, we'll calculate the variance using the following formula:

$$\sigma_1^2 = avg(X'_1 * X'_1), \sigma_2^2 = avg(X'_2 * X'_2)$$

This is the average of the square of the zero mean feature, which is the feature that we subtracted on the previous step. We'll then calculate the standard deviation, which is given as follows:

$$X''_1 = X'_1 - \sqrt{\sigma_1^2}, X''_2 = X'_2 - \sqrt{\sigma_1^2}$$

This is graphically represented as follows:

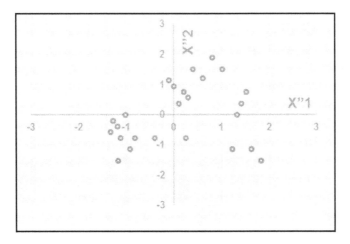

Notice how, in this graph, X_1 is taking almost approximately the same variance as X_2.

Normalizing the data helps the neural network to work faster. If we plot the weights and the cost function j for normalized data, we'll get a three-dimensional, non-regular screenshot as follows:

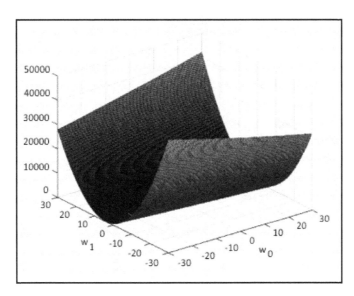

If we plot the contour in a two-dimensional plane, it may look something like the following skew screenshot:

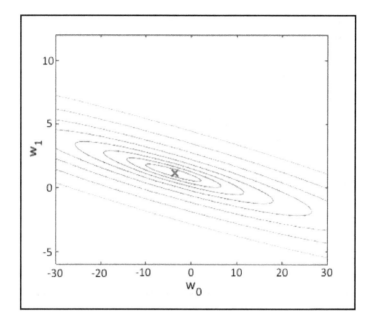

Observe that the model may take different times to go to the minimum; that is, the red point marked in the plot.

If we consider this example, we can see that the cost values are oscillating between a different range of values, therefore taking a lot of time to go to the minimum.

To reduce the effect of the oscillating values, sometimes we need to lower the alpha learning rate, which means that we take even smaller steps. The reason we lower the learning rate is to avoid a convergence. Converging is like taking these kinds of values and never reaching the minimum value, as shown in the following plot:

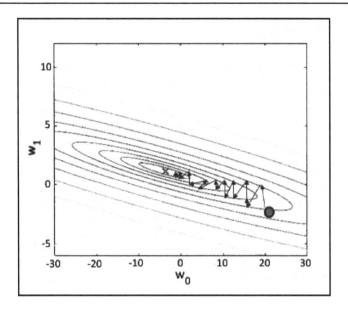

Plotting the same data with normalization will give you a graph as follows:

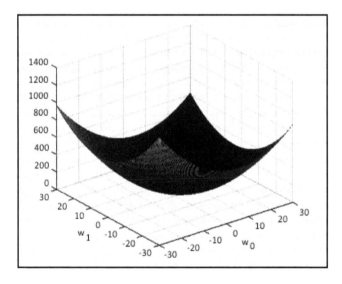

So we get a model that is regular or spherical in shape, and if we plot it in a two-dimensional plane, it will give a more rounded graph:

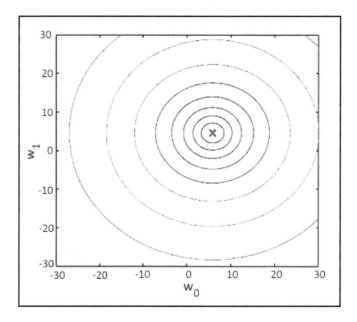

Here, regardless of where you initialize the data, it will take the same time to get to the minimum point. Look at the following diagram; you can see that the values are stable:

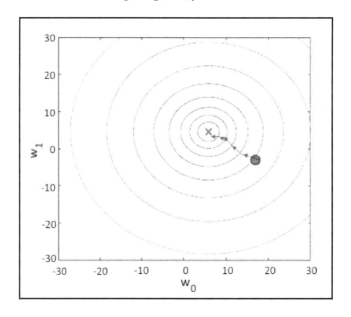

I think it is now safe to conclude that normalizing the data is very important and harmless. So, if you are not sure whether to do it or not, it's always a better idea to do it than avoid it.

Initializing the weights

We are already aware that we have no weight values at the beginning. In order to solve that problem, we will initialize the weights with random non-zero values. This might work well, but here, we are going to look at how initializing weights greatly impacts the learning time of our neural network.

Suppose we have a deep neural network with many hidden layers, and each of these high layers is connected to two neurons. For the sake of simplicity, we'll not take the sigmoid function but the identity activation function, which simply leaves the input untouched. The value is given by **F(z),** or simply **Z**:

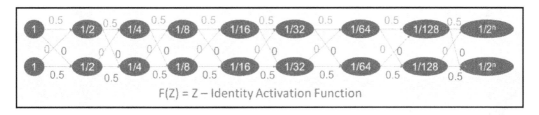

F(Z) = Z – Identity Activation Function

Assume that we have weights as depicted in the previous diagram. Calculating the Z at the hidden layer and the neuron or the activation values are the same because of the identity function. The first neuron in the first hidden layer will be *1*0.5+1*0*, which is 0.5. The same applies for the second neuron. When we move to the second hidden layer, the value of Z for this second hidden layer is *0.5 *0.5+0.5 *0*, which gives us 0.25 or 1/4; if we continue the same logic, we'll have 1/8, 1/16, and so on, until we have the formula $(1/2)^n$. What this tells us is that the deeper our neural network becomes, the smaller this activation value gets. This concept is also called the vanishing gradient. Originally, the concept referred to the gradient rather than activation values, but we can easily adapt it to gradients and the concept holds the same. If we replace the 0.5 with a 1.5, then we will have $(1.5)^n$ in the end, which tells us that the deeper our neural network gets, the greater the activation function becomes. This is known as the exploding gradient values.

In order to avoid both situations, we may want to replace the zero value with a 0.5. If we do that, the first neuron in the first hidden layer will have the value *1*0.5+1*0.5*, which is equal to 1. This does not really help our cause because our output is then equal to the input, so maybe we can slightly modify to have not 0.5, but a random value that is as near to 0.5 as possible.

In a way, we would like to have weights valued with a variance of 0.5. More formally, we want the variance of the weights to be 1 divided by the number of neurons in the previous layer, which is mathematically expressed as follows:

$$V(W^l) = \frac{1}{n^{l-1}}$$

To obtain the actual values, we need to multiply the square root of the variance formula to a normal distribution of random values. This is known as the Xavier initialization:

$$V(W^l) = \frac{1}{n^{l-1}}, W^l = \sqrt{\frac{2}{n^{l-1}}} * randn$$

If we replace the 1 with 2 in this formula, we will have even greater performance for our neural network. It'll converge faster to the minimum.

We may also find different versions of the formula. One of them is the following:

$$W^l = \sqrt{\frac{2}{n^l * n^{l-1}}} * randn$$

It modifies the term to have the multiplication of the number of neurons in the actual layer with the number of neurons in the previous layer.

Activation functions

We've learned about the sigmoid function so far, but it is used comparatively less in the modern era of deep learning. The reason for this is because the tanh function works much better than the sigmoid function. The tanh function is grahically represented as follows:

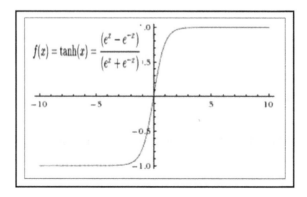

If you look at the graph, you can see that this function looks similar to the sigmoid function, but is centered at the zero. The reason it works better is because it's easier to center your data around 0 than around 0.5.

However, they both share a downside: when the weights become bigger or smaller, this slope in the graph becomes smaller, to almost zero, and that slows down our neural network a lot. In order to overcome this, we have the ReLU function, which always guarantees a slope.

The ReLU function is one of the reasons we can afford to have deeper neural networks with high efficiency. It has also become the default application for all neural networks. The ReLU function is graphically represented as follows:

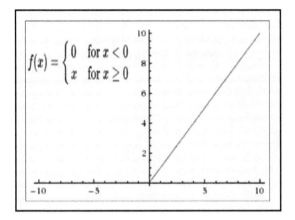

A small modification to the ReLU function, will lead us to the leaky ReLU function that is shown in the next graph; here, instead of taking zero, it takes a small value:

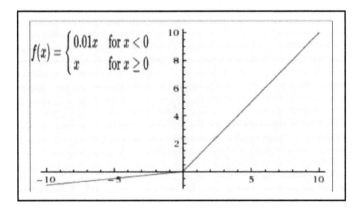

So sometimes, this works better than the ReLU function but most of the time, actually a ReLU function works just fine.

Optimizing algorithms

In the previous section, we learned how to normalize the data and initialize the weights, along with choosing a good activation function that can dramatically speed up neural network learning time.

In this section, we'll take a step further by optimizing our algorithm and the way we update the weights in a backward pass.

To do this, we need to revisit how a neural network learns. We begin with training data of size *m*, and each of the examples depicted in this section has *n* features, and for each of the examples, we also have its corresponding prediction value:

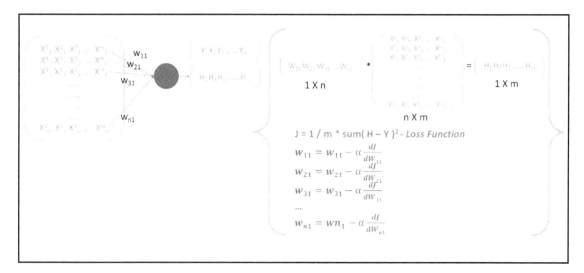

What we want is a neural network to learn from these examples to predict the results for its own examples. The first step is to do the forward pass with just a multiplication with these *m* examples. This is done using matrices for efficiency, because all this multiplication can be done in parallel and thus we can make good use of the GPU and CPU power. This will produce the *m* hypothesis. After that, it's time to see how good our hypothesis is doing compared to real values and hypothetical ones. This is done by using the cost function, which is the averaging difference between the hypothesis and all the examples.

After this, we will do the backward pass, where we simply update the weight in such a way that the next time we run this network, we'll have a better hypothesis. This is done by calculating the derivative of the cost function by all the weights, and subtracting this from the current weights value. If we normalize our data and initialize it with Xavier, as depicted in the following diagram, we notice the progress to the minimum value where the hypothesis is almost equal to the real value:

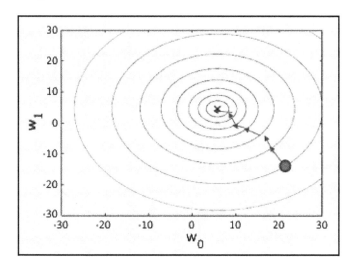

One forward pass and its simultaneous backward pass through the data is called an epoch. We need approximately 100 to 150 epochs to go to the minimum value.

Previously, we had a lower number of examples and it was alright to run the network for 100-150 epochs. But these days, with 1 million examples in a dataset, the amount of time consumed to run the network or even to move from one step to the other will be ridiculously long. Of course, the reason for this is that we are multiplying each weight with a matrix consisting of 1 million examples here. This will obviously slow down the learning drastically. To make it worse, this would happen for 100-150 epochs, which makes this practically impossible.

One way to improve this is to update the weights for each example, instead of waiting until the network has seen all 1 million of examples. The network will now look as follows:

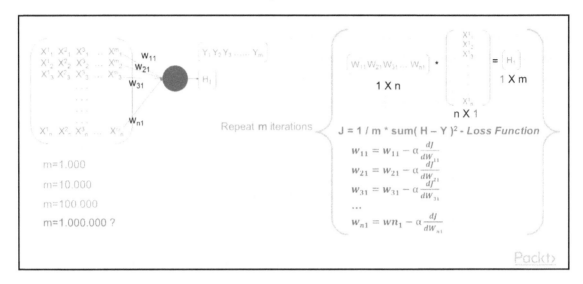

When initialized on Xavier, this is what it looks as in following diagram:

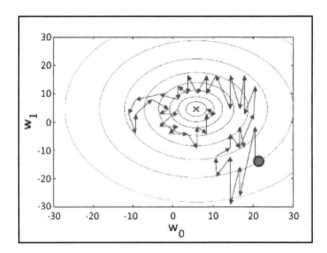

The positive aspect of this is that we get to the minimum point really quick. The downside of this is that the progress is really noisy. We have a lot of oscillating values and sometimes the point does not move toward the minimum point, and instead moves backward.

This is not a huge obstacle as it can be resolved to a certain extent by reducing the α learning rate. Thus, we can attain better results.

The greatest disadvantage of this method is that we actually do not make appropriate use of the parallelism and the great processing power of the CPUs and GPUs, as we are multiplying the weights with just one example.

In order to reap the benefits of both the methods, we can use a **mini-batch gradient descent,** which, instead of using 1 or 1 million examples, uses k-number of examples. The value of the k-number can be more or less; it could be 500, 1,000, or 32. It is a value that would make the matrix big enough to use the maximum processing power of GPUs or even CPUs. If we initialize Xavier, it looks something like the following:

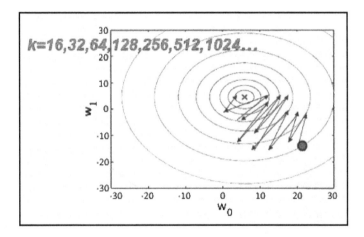

Even here, we observe that the progress to the center is not as noisy as in the stochastic gradient distant with the one example we have seen so far.

If we take k as the size of the example or the mini-batch gradient before updating the weights, then it will take us m/k iterations to complete sifting through all the data; that is, to do one epoch. The normally-used k-values are 16, 32, 64,...1,024. Basically, just a power of two, as it provides good results.

In general cases, we need several epochs to go to the minimum point, which means for one epoch, we need m/k iterations to go through all the data. The number of epochs varies from case to case; we just need to see how our neural network progresses.

The mini-batch gradient descent is the default choice and is really efficient in production. Even if the oscillating values were improved, they were quite evident, so let's see how we can improve this.

Let's suppose that we have the data with oscillating values, as depicted in the following graph:

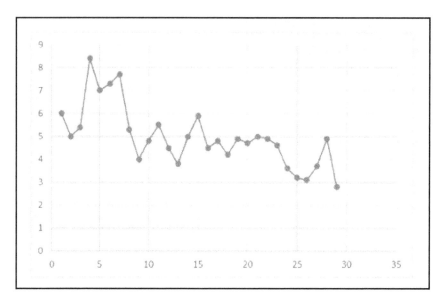

The aim is to have a smooth curve to our data, instead of these oscillating values. To do this, we could trust a new common example, but it would be better to take the average of the new example and an older example, and instead trust that average. Of course, we don't want a simple average here, we just want more recent values to have a greater impact on our output. The following mathematical function, which is the equation for expanded weighted average, helps us do this:

$$V_t = \beta * V_{t-1} + (1 + \beta) * V_t$$

In order to understand why this works, let us consider the example for V_3. The equation for V_3, V_2, and V_1, and V_0 will be as follows:

$$V_3 = \beta * V_2 + (1 - \beta) * V_3$$

Substitute the values of V_1 and V_2 in the equation of V_3, which is mathematically shown as follows:

$$V_3 = \beta * V_1 + (1 - \beta) * V_2$$

$$V_3 = \beta * V_0 + (1 - \beta) * V_1$$

$$V_0 = 0$$

Substituting these values, we get the following:

$$V_3 = \beta^2 * (1 - \beta) * V_1 + \beta * (1 - \beta) * V_2 + (1 - \beta) * V_3$$

$$V_3 = 0.125 * (V_1) + 0.25 * V_2 + 0.5 * V_3$$

Observe that the weights here are different from each of these examples. If we replace the value of β with 0.5, we can see the gradual decrease in the weights across the equation. This gives us the possibility to have a weighted average, such that values that are not important have smaller weights, leading it to contribute less to the overall average.

It just so happens that this β greatly affects the value of the result. Let us look at a comparative analysis of various values of β. If β= **0.2, 0.5, 0.7,** and **0.9**, here is what your graph will look like:

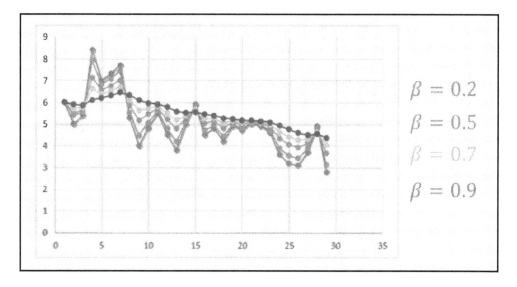

When the value is β is **0.2**, the orange line in the graph depicting the output of β is almost identical to the blue line. As the value of β is increased, we can see that the output has fewer oscillations and a smoother curve.

Let's understand how to use this technique to smooth out the updates of the weights in the network. Instead of taking on the form of oscillating values, we want a more linear update:

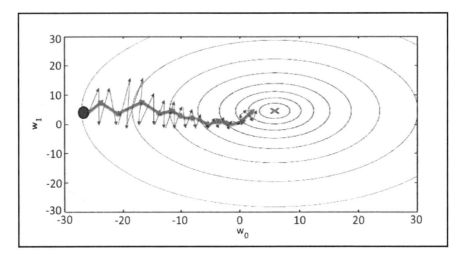

The first step is to modify the way we update the weights, instead of immediately trusting the derivative cost function with a weight with the help of the V_t equation. Using all the equations described previously, we make our results more linear in nature.

There are two more ways to smooth out oscillations:

- **RSMprop**: This has the same core concept and intuition as the method explained previously. It is mathematically expressed as follows:

RMSProp

$$S_0 = 0$$

$$S_t = \beta * S_{t-1} + (1 - \beta) * \left(\frac{dJ}{dW_{xy}}\right)^2$$

$$w_{xy} = wxy - \alpha\frac{dJ}{dW_{xy}} \qquad w_{xy} = wxy - \alpha * \frac{\frac{dJ}{dw_{xy}}}{\sqrt{S_t}}$$

In this case, instead of the derivative, we have to use a squared derivative. Similarly, we do not take the derivative of the cost value but instead divide it with the square root of S_t. This only works because we have V_1 with a large value, thus, automatically increasing the value of S_t. We divide the cost function by a large value to get smaller values and smooth out the oscillations.

- **ADAM**: The ADAM method is simply a merge of what we've seen so far. We calculate the value of V_t and S_t using the following formulas:

$$V_0 = 0 \quad S_0 = 0$$

$$V_t = \beta * V_{t-1} + (1 - \beta) * \frac{dJ}{dW_{xy}} \qquad S_t = \beta_2 * S_{t-1} + (1 - \beta_2) * \left(\frac{dJ}{dW_{xy}}\right)^2$$

Instead of trusting a new example, we update the weights using this formula:

$$w_{xy} = wxy - \alpha \frac{dJ}{dW_{xy}} \qquad w_{xy} = wxy - \alpha * \frac{V_t}{\sqrt{S_t}}$$

Here, V_t is divided by the square root of S_t.

ADAM is a really helpful technique and is used widely across neural networks.

Fortunately, most of the time, we don't need really to vary the β and β_2 parameters. The default parameters work just fine. β varies rarely from 0.85 to 0.9. β_2 almost never changes and stays constant at 0.999.

Configuring the training parameters of the neural network

Through the course of this chapter, we have learned several optimization techniques. These, in combination with several other parameters, can help speed up the learning time of our neural network.

In this section of the chapter, we are going to look at a range of parameters, focus on the parameters that are most likely to produce good results when changed, and learn how to tune these parameters to obtain the the best possible outcome.

Here are the parameters that we have looked at so far:

- **Data input normalization**: Data input normalization is more of a preprocessing technique than it is a parameter. We mention it on this list because it is, in a manner of speaking, a mandatory step. The second reason data input normalization belongs in this list is merely because it is essential for batch normalization. Batch normalization not only normalizes the input, but also the hidden layer inputs γ, β and the Z-values as we have observed in the previous sections. This method has led the neural network to learn how to normalize the hidden layer input according to the best bit. Fortunately, we do not need to worry about the γ and β parameter, as the network learns these values automatically.

- α **learning rate**: The one parameter that always needs attention is the α learning rate. As stated in the last section of this chapter, the α learning rate defines how quickly our neural network will learn, and usually it takes values such as -0.1, 0.01,0.001,0.00001, and 0.000001. We also saw how a neural network organizes matrices for greater performance. This is only because matrix operations offer a high level of parallelism.

- **Mini-batch size and the number of epochs**: The mini-batch size is the number of inputs that can be fed to the neural network before the weights are updated or before moving toward the minimum. The mini-batch size, therefore, directly affects the level of parallelism. The batch size depends on the hardware used and is defined as k-number of CPU cores or GPU units. The batch size for a CPU core could be 4, 8, 16, or maybe 32, depending on the hardware. For a GPU, this value is much greater, such as 256, or maybe 512, or even 1,024, depending on the model of the graphic card.

- **The number of neurons in the hidden layer**: This value increases the number of weights and the weight combinations, therefore enabling us to create and learn complex models, which in turn helps us solve complex problems. The reason we find this parameter so far down the list is because most of the time this number can be taken from literature and well-known architectures, so we don't have to tune this ourselves. There maybe a rare few cases where we would need to change this value based on our personal needs. This number could vary from hundreds to thousands; some deep networks have 9,000 neurons in the hidden layer.

- **The number of hidden layers**: Increasing the number of hidden layers would lead to a dramatic increase in the number of weights, since it would actually define how deep the neural network is. The number of hidden layers can vary from 2 to 22 to 152, where 2 would be the simplest network and 152 hidden layers would be a really deep neural network. During the course of this book, we will take a look at creating a deep neural network using transfer learning.
- α **learning rate decay**: The α learning rate decay is a technique to load the α learning rate as we train our neural network for longer periods of time. The reason we want to implement this is because when we use the mini-batch gradient descent; we do not go straight to the minimum value. The oscillating values and the nature of the batch itself lead us to not consider the example itself, but just a subset of it. To lower this value, we use a simple formula:

$$\frac{1}{1 + decay_r ate * epochN} * \alpha$$

Observe how when the epoch number increases, the value of α learning rate decay becomes less than 1, but when multiplied by α, we reduce the effect of these values. The significance of the decay rate in this formula is to just accelerate the reduction of this alpha when the epoch number increases.

- β **momentum parameter**: The β momentum parameter lies in the range of 0.8 to 0.95. This parameter rarely needs to be tuned.
- **ADAM** $\beta1$, $\beta2$, ϵ: ADAM almost never needs tuning.

This list is ordered in a manner such that the first one has more of an effect on the outcome.

One of the things that is important when choosing the parameter values is carefully picking the scale. Consider an example where we have to set the number of neurons in the hidden layers, and by intuition, this number lies between 100 to 200. The reasonable thing to do is to uniformly and randomly pick a number in this segment or in this range of values. Unfortunately, this does not work for all the parameters.

To decide the α learning rate, let us begin by assuming that the best value will likely be in the range of 0.1 to 1; in the image below, notice how 90% of our resources go to choosing values between **0.1** and **1**. This does not sound right, since only 10% go to finding values in the remaining three ranges, 0.001-0.01-0.1. But since we do not have any preference, the values can be found equally in all these four ranges:

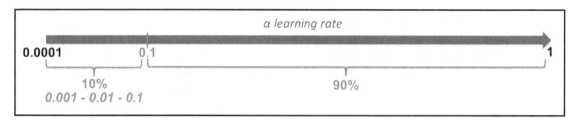

It would make sense to divide the segment into four equal parts and ranges and look for our value, uniformly and randomly. One way to do that efficiently is to look for random values in the range of -4 to 0, using the following code:

After this, we can return to the original scale by using 10 to the power of whatever this function produces as a value. Calling the same line of code four times, once for each segment, will work just fine:

```
ThreadLocalRandom.current().nextDouble(-4, 0);
```

Let us begin exploring the process of selecting the parameters. We have several parameters to tune, so the process may look like this random grid here:

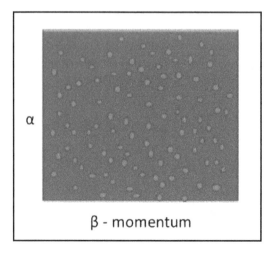

For one random value of alpha, we can try different beta values and vice versa. In practice, we have more than two values. Look at the following block:

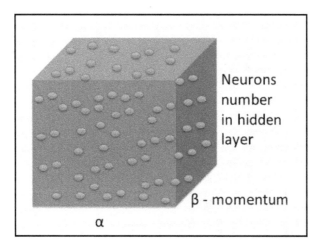

You can pick one random alpha, try several beta values, and then, for each of these beta values, you try varying the number of neurons in the hidden layers. This process can be adopted for an even greater number of parameters, such as four, five, and so on.

The other thing that can help is a more varied version of the original process:

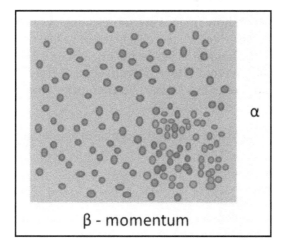

During the fine-tuning of the parameters, we can observe that the highlighted bunch of values actually produce a better output. We look at this closely:

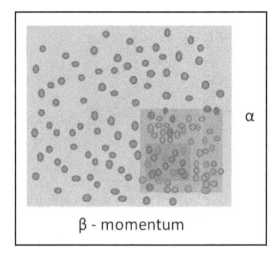

We can continue to do this until we have the required results.

Representing images and outputs

This section mainly focuses on how images are represented on a computer and how to feed this to the neural network. Based on what we've learned so far, neural networks predict only binary classes, where the answer is yes or no, or right or wrong. Consider the example of predicting whether a patient would have heart disease or not. The answer to this is binary in nature—yes or no. We will now learn to train our neural network to predict multiple classes using softmax.

A computer perceives an image as a two-dimensional matrix of numbers. Look at the following diagram:

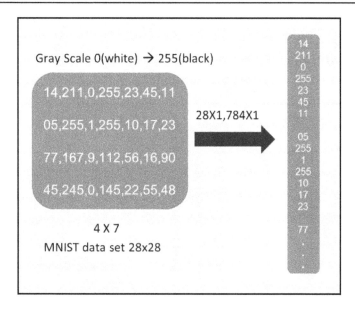

These numbers make little sense to us, but to a computer they mean everything. For a black-and-white image, each of these pixel values depicts the intensity of the light, so zero means white, and as we move closer to the number 255, the pixel gets darker. In this case, we considered an image with the dimensions 4 x 7. Images of the MNIST database are actually 28 x 28 in size. In order to make an image ready for processing, we need to transform it to a one-dimensional vector, which means that a 28 x 28 image will be transformed to 784 x 1 image and a 4 x 7 image to a 28 x 1.

Notice now how this one-dimensional vector is no different from a binary class case. Each of these pixels now is just a feature for a computer vision application. We can, of course, add k-images representations, if we choose a mini-batch gradient descent, which would process k-images in parallel.

When using Java, the values are parameters and their significance is inverse in nature. Here, 0 means black and 255 means white. In order to correctly depict an MNIST dataset image using Java, we need to use the $255 - V_{ij}$ formula, where V_{ij} is the value of the pixel. This happens to be the case with most languages similar to Java:

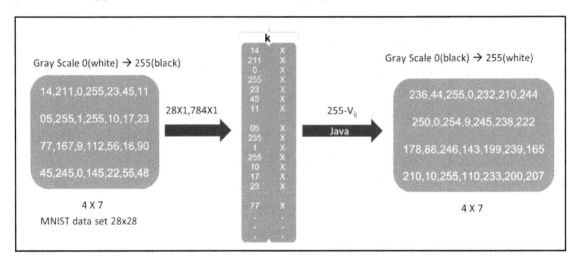

For colored images, consider an RGB-color JPG, which has a size of 260 x 194 pixels. The computer will see it as a three-dimensional matrix of numbers. Specifically, it will see it as 260 x 194 x 3. Each of the dimensions represents the intensity of the red color, the green color, and the blue color:

So if we take the red example, 0 means the color black, and 255 will be completely red. The same logic applies to the green and the blue colors. We need to transform the three-dimensional matrix to a one-dimensional vector, just as we did previously:

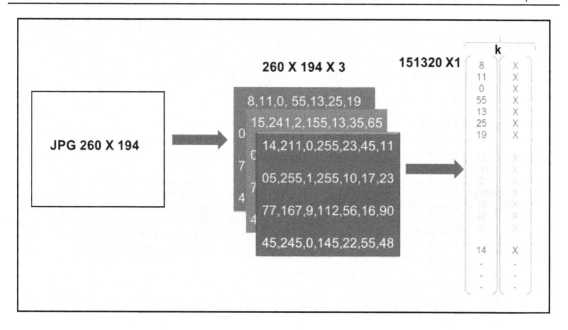

We can also add k-images by choosing mini-batch gradient descent and processing k-images in parallel.

Notice how the number of features dramatically increases for color images, from 784 to 150,000 features. Due to this, the processing time of the image increases drastically, which is where we need to implement techniques to increase the speed of our model.

Multiclass classification

So far, we've seen multiple activation functions, but the one thing that remains constant is the limitation that they can provide only two classes, 0 or 1. Consider the heart disease example:

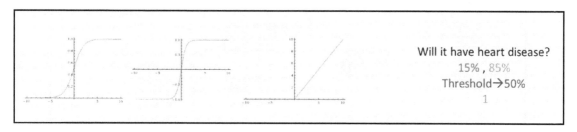

The neural network predicted 15% not having heart disease and 85% having heart disease, and we set the threshold to 50%. This implies that as soon as one of these percentages exceeds the threshold, we output its index, which would be 0 or 1. In this example, obviously 85% is greater than 50%, so we will output **1**, meaning that this person will not have heart disease in the future.

These days, neural networks can actually predict thousands of classes. In the case of ImageNet, we can predict thousands of images. We do this by labeling our images with more than just **0** and **1**. Look at the following photos:

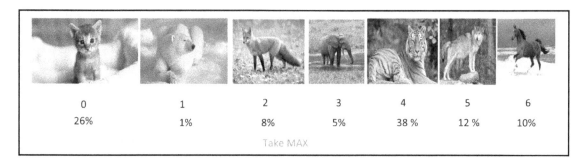

0	1	2	3	4	5	6
26%	1%	8%	5%	38 %	12 %	10%

Take MAX

Here, we label the photos from 0 to 6 and let the neural network assign each image some percentage. In this case, we consider the maximum, which would be 38%. The neural network will then give us image 4 as the output. Notice how the sum of these percentages will be 100%.

Let us now move into implementing the multiclass classification. Here is what we have seen so far:

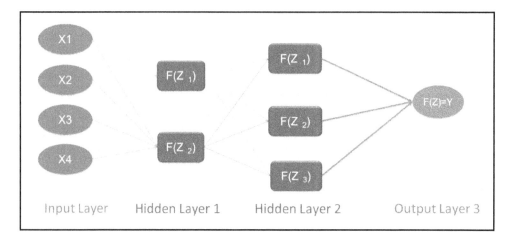

This is a neural network containing an activation function in the outer layer. Let us replace this activation function with three nodes, assuming we need to predict three classes instead of two:

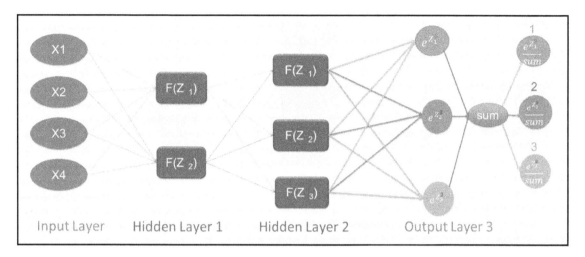

Each of these nodes will have a different function, which will be e^z. Thus, we will have z_1, z_2, and z_3, sum up this e^z, and conclude by dividing e^z by the sum of the three values. This step of division is just to make sure that the sum of these percentages will be 100%.

Consider an example where z_1 is 5, making $e^{z_1^3}$ equal to 148.4. z_2 is 2, which makes $e^{z_2^3}$ equal to 7.4. Similarly, z_3 can be set to -1 and $e^{z_3^3}$ will be equal to 0.4. The sum of these values is 156.2. The next step, as discussed, is dividing each of these values by the sum to attain the final percentages.

For class 1, we get 95%, class 2 gives us 4.7%, and class 3 gives us 0.3%.

As logic dictates, the neural network will choose class 1 as the outcome. And since 95% is much greater than 50%, this is what we will choose as a threshold.

Here is what our final neural network looks like:

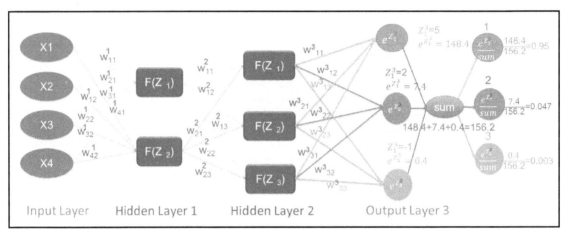

The weights depicted by the subscript 1 are going to the hidden layer 1, and the weights depicted by the subscript 2 are for the hidden layer 2.

The Z values are the sum of multiplication of the inputs with the weights, which, in this case, is the sum of the multiplication of the activation function with the weights.

In reality, we have another weight called the bias, b, which is added to the older value Z. The following diagram should help you understand this better:

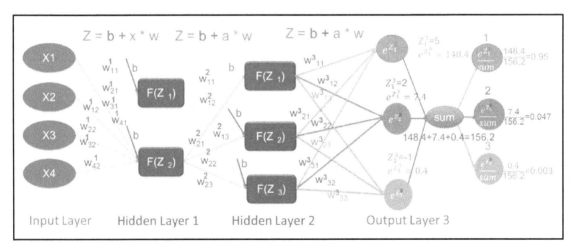

The bias weight is updated in the same way as the v weight.

Building a handwritten digit recognizer

By building a handwritten digit recognizer in a Java application, we will practically implement most of the techniques and optimizations learned so far. The application is built using the open source Java framework, Deeplearning4j. The dataset used is the classic MNIST database of handwritten digits. (http://yann.lecun.com/exdb/mnist/). The training dataset is oversized, having 60,000 images, while the test data set contains 10,000 images. The images are 28 x 28 in size and grayscale in terms of terms.

As a part of the application that we will be creating in this section, we will implement a graphical user interface, where you can draw digits and get a neural network to recognize the digit.

Jumping straight into the code, let's observe how to implement a neural network in Java. We begin with the parameters; the first one is the output. Since we have 0 to 9 digits, we have 10 classes:

```
/**
    * Number prediction classes.
    * We have 0-9 digits so 10 classes in total.
    */
private static final int OUTPUT = 10;
```

We have the mini-batch size, which is the number of images we see before updating the weights or the number of images we'll process in parallel:

```
/**
 * Mini batch gradient descent size or number of matrices processed in
parallel.
 * For CORE-I7 16 is good for GPU please change to 128 and up
 */
 private static final int MINI_BATCH_SIZE = 16;// Number of training epochs
/**
 * Number of total traverses through data.
 * with 5 epochs we will have 5/@MINI_BATCH_SIZE iterations or weights
updates
 */
 private static final int EPOCHS = 5;
```

When we consider this for a CPU, the batch size of 16 is alright, but for GPUs, this needs to change according to the GPU power. One epoch is fulfilled when we traverse all the data.

The learning rate is quite important, because having a very low value will slow down the learning, and having bigger values of the learning rate will cause the neural network to actually diverge:

```
/**
 * The alpha learning rate defining the size of step towards the minimum
 */
private static final double LEARNING_RATE = 0.01;
```

To understand this in detail, in the latter half of this section, we will simulate a case where we diverge by changing the learning rate. Fortunately, as part of this example, we need not handle the reading, transferring, or normalizing of the pixels from the MNIST dataset. We do not need to concern ourselves with transforming the data to a one-dimensional vector to fit to the neural network. This is because everything is encapsulated and offered by Deeplearning4j.

Under the object **dataset iterator,** we need to specify the batch size and whether we are going to use it for training or testing, which will help classify whether we need to load 60,000 images from the training dataset, or 10,000 from the testing dataset:

```
public void train() throws Exception {
/*
 Create an iterator using the batch size for one iteration
 */
 log.info("Load data....");
 DataSetIterator mnistTrain = new MnistDataSetIterator(MINI_BATCH_SIZE,
true, SEED);
/*
 Construct the neural neural
 */
 log.info("Build model....");

 MultiLayerConfiguration conf = new NeuralNetConfiguration.Builder()
 .seed(SEED)
 .learningRate(LEARNING_RATE)
 .weightInit(WeightInit.XAVIER)
 //NESTEROVS is referring to gradient descent with momentum
 .updater(Updater.NESTEROVS)
 .list()
```

Let's get started with building a neural network. We've specified the learning rate, and initialized the weight according to Xavier, which we have learned in the previous sections. The updater in the code is actually just the optimization algorithm for updating the weights with a gradient descent. The NESTEROVS is basically the gradient descent with momentum that we're already familiar with.

Let's look into the code to understand the updater better. We look at the two formulas that are actually not different from what we have already explored.

We configure the input layer, hidden layers, and the output. Configuration of the input layer is quite easy; we just need to multiply the width and the weight and we have this one-dimensional vector size. The next step in the code is to define the hidden layers. We have two hidden layers, actually: one with 128 neurons and one with 64 neurons, both having an activation function because of its high efficiency.

Just to switch things up a bit, we could try out different values, especially those defined by the `MNIST` dataset web page. Despite that, the values chosen here are quite efficient, with less training time and good accuracy.

The output layer, which uses the softmax, because we need ten classes and not 2, we also have the cost function. The details for this may vary from what we have seen previously. This function measures the performance of the hypothetical values against the real values.

We then initialize and define the function, as we want to see the cost function for every 100 iterations. The `model.fit (minstTrain)` is very important, because this actually works iteration by iteration, as defined by many, it traverses all the data. After this, we have executed one epoch and the neural network has learned to use good weights.

Testing the performance of the neural network

To test the accuracy of the network, we construct another dataset for testing. We evaluate this model with what we've learned so far and print the statistics. If the accuracy of the network is more than 97%, we stop there and save the model to use for the graphical user interface that we will study later on. Execute the following code:

```
if (mnistTest == null) {
  mnistTest = new MnistDataSetIterator(MINI_BATCH_SIZE, false, SEED);
  }
```

The cost function is being printed and if you observe it closely, it gradually decreases through the iterations. From time to time, we have a peak in the value of the cost function. This is a characteristic of the mini-batch gradient descent. The final output of the first epoch shows us that the model has 96% accuracy just for one epoch, which is great. This means the neural network is learning fast.

In most cases, it does not work like this and we need to tune our network for a long time before we obtain the output we want. Let's look at the output of the second epoch:

```
# of classes:        10
Accuracy:            0.9731
Precision:           0.9731
Recall:              0.9728
F1 Score:            0.9729
Precision, recall & F1: macro-averaged (equally weighted avg. of 10 classes)
================================================================================
[2018-04-07 01:55:04]Saving model at C:\devSources\ComputerVision\HandWrittenDigitReco
[2018-04-07 01:55:04]Congratulations,the desired score found,!
[2018-04-07 01:55:04]***************Example finished********************

Process finished with exit code 0
```

We obtain an accuracy of more than 97% in just two epochs.

Another aspect that we need to draw our attention to is how a simple model is achieving really great results. This is a part of the reason why deep learning is taking off. It is easy to obtain good results, and it is easy to work with.

As mentioned before, let's look at a case of disconverging by increasing the learning rate to 0.6:

```
private static final double LEARNING_RATE = 0.01;

/**
 * https://en.wikipedia.org/wiki/Random_seed
 */
private static final int SEED = 123;
private static final int IMAGE_WIDTH = 28;
private static final int IMAGE_HEIGHT = 28;
```

If we now run the network, we will observe that the cost function will continue to increase with no signs of decreasing. The accuracy is also affected greatly. The cost function for one epoch almost stays the same, despite having 3,000 iterations. The final accuracy of the model is approximately 10%, which is a clear indication that this is not the best method.

Let's run the application for various digits and see how it works. Let's begin with the number **3**:

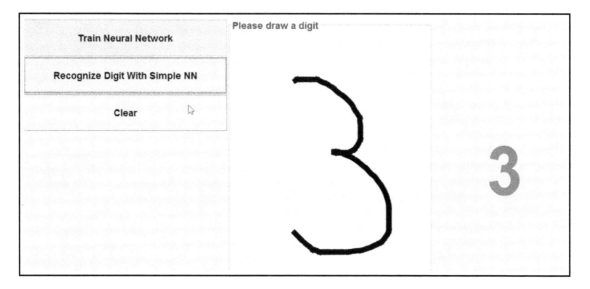

The output is accurate. Run this for any of the numbers that lie between Zero to nine and check whether your model is working accurately.

Also, keep in mind that the model is not perfect yet-we shall improve this with CNN architectures in the next chapter. They offer state-of-the-art techniques and high accuracy, and we should be able to achieve an accuracy of 99%.

Summary

In this chapter, we have covered a vast variety of topics. We began by understanding the computer state vision and the importance of data in deep learning algorithms. We explored neural networks and built a neural network.

We also looked at how a neural network learns. The importance of organizing data and effective training techniques were also looked at. Lastly, we built a handwritten digit recognizer.

In the next chapter, we will look at edge detection and build a model using it.

2
Convolutional Neural Network Architectures

In this chapter, we'll explore edge detection as one of the most fundamental and widely-used techniques in computer vision. Then, we'll look at edge detection in action, using a number of features and images, by building a Java application that detects edges on different images. As a next step, we'll detail how to use edge detection or convolution with colored RGB images so that we can capture even more features from images. We'll present them using several parameters, which will enable us to control the output of the convolution operation. Then, we'll look at a slightly different type of filter, the pooling layers, and one of the most frequently used: the max pooling layer. After that, we'll put all the pieces together for the purpose of building and training a convolution neural network. Finally, we'll use the convolution architecture, as we did in the previous chapter, to optimize handwritten digit recognition with an accuracy of 99.95%.

We will cover the following topics in this chapter:

- Understanding edge detection
- Building a Java edge detection application
- Convolution on RGB images
- Working with convolutional layers' parameters
- Pooling layers
- Building and training a convolutional neural network
- Improving the handwritten digit recognition application

Understanding edge detection

Although neural networks are really powerful models, computer vision is a complex problem to solve, since we need more specialized feature detectors for images. In this section, we'll explore edge detection as one of the fundamental techniques in computer vision for neural network architectures. Then, we'll visit horizontal and vertical edge detection, and finally, we'll understand why edge detection is doing so well.

What is edge detection?

Edges are the pixels where the sight color of the pixels dramatically changes from one side to the other. For example, let's look at the following image:

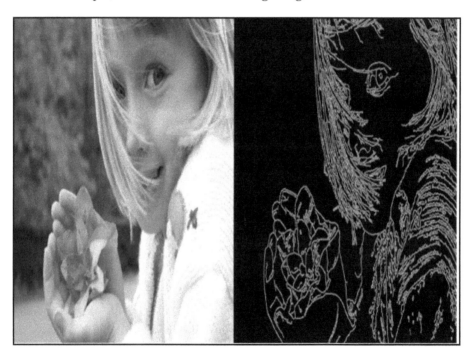

The edges in the preceding screenshot are where the pixel color changes dramatically, such as from green to the hair color—blonde. For the flower, it will be exactly where the color will dramatically change for the first time from green to pink. On the right-hand side, we can see the output that we'll get after running the edge detection application. Hence, we can see the hands, the flower, the colors, the eye, and places where the color changes from up to down.

Vertical edge detection

Now, let's see how we can detect edges in a computer system where images actually are just metrics with numbers. Let's suppose we have this screenshot:

We have white on the left and black on the right. This will be represented in Java, for example, as follows:

255	255	255	10	10	10
255	255	255	10	10	10
255	255	255	10	10	10
255	255	255	10	10	10
255	255	255	10	10	10
255	255	255	10	10	10
255	255	255	10	10	10
255	255	255	10	10	10

255 will be white, and **10** will be black.

Then, we'll define a convolution operation with a small matrix, which will be called the **Vertical Filter**:

255	255	255	10	10	10
255	255	255	10	10	10
255	255	255	10	10	10
255	255	255	10	10	10
255	255	255	10	10	10
255	255	255	10	10	10
255	255	255	10	10	10
255	255	255	10	10	10

$*$

1	0	-1
1	0	-1
1	0	-1

Vertical Filter

The vertical filter will move in this big matrix, starting in the top-left corner:

255	255	255	10	10	10
255	255	255	10	10	10
255	255	255	10	10	10
255	255	255	10	10	10
255	255	255	10	10	10
255	255	255	10	10	10
255	255	255	10	10	10
255	255	255	10	10	10

$*$

1	0	-1
1	0	-1
1	0	-1

Vertical Filter

Then, it will move to the right:

255	255	255	10	10	10
255	255	255	10	10	10
255	255	255	10	10	10
255	255	255	10	10	10
255	255	255	10	10	10
255	255	255	10	10	10
255	255	255	10	10	10
255	255	255	10	10	10

$*$

1	0	-1
1	0	-1
1	0	-1

Vertical Filter

It will keep moving this way until there are no movements; that is; until the starting edge meets the ending edge.

Then it will go down, and move to the right again:

255	255	255	10	10	10
255	255	255	10	10	10
255	255	255	10	10	10
255	255	255	10	10	10
255	255	255	10	10	10
255	255	255	10	10	10
255	255	255	10	10	10
255	255	255	10	10	10

$*$

1	0	-1
1	0	-1
1	0	-1

Vertical Filter

Then it will move down and right, until we reach the bottom-right corner. Let's see more clearly how the convolution will be done in this matrix.

First, let's go to the top-left corner, and multiply these cells together:

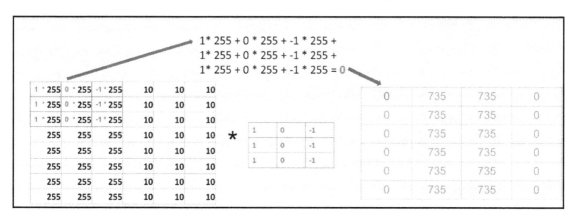

If we take the block highlighted in the screenshot, we'll multiply **1** by **255**, add **0** multiplied by **255**, and then subtract **1** multiplied by **255**. We'll add them together and then we'll add this to the second row result and the third row result, and all these produce one value, which is zero, and we put this **0** in the top-left corner of the output matrix, as shown in the screenshot.

Then, we move one square to the right, and we do the same thing again:

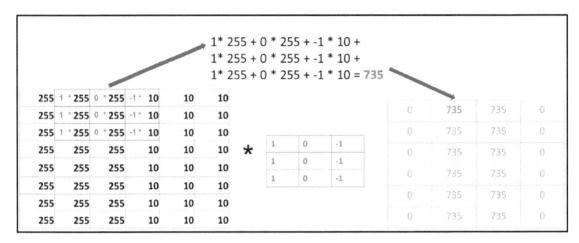

Each of these cells will be multiplied by the cells in the vertical filter; this time we have **735**, and we'll put it in the second cell, but we have a different value here.

Then, we'll move one to the right, where we have **735** again:

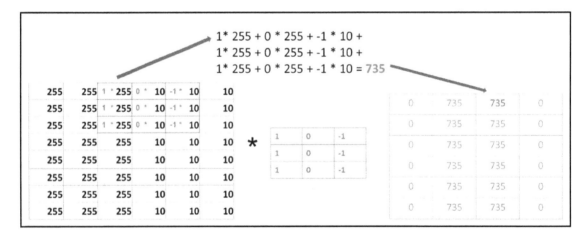

And moving right one more time, we have **0**:

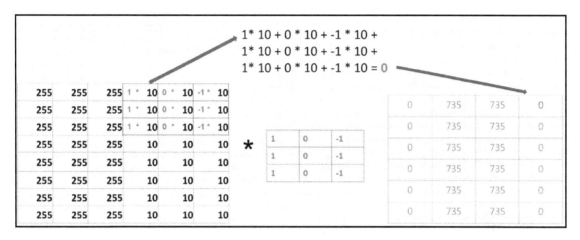

Since we can't move to the right any more, we move down. We'll perform the same operation as before. We have **0**, but we put it now on the second row, since we have completed the first row:

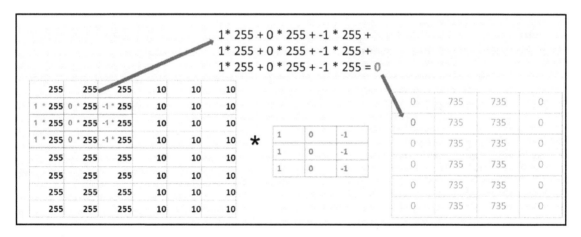

We now move one to the right again, and we put it here, as shown in the following screenshot:

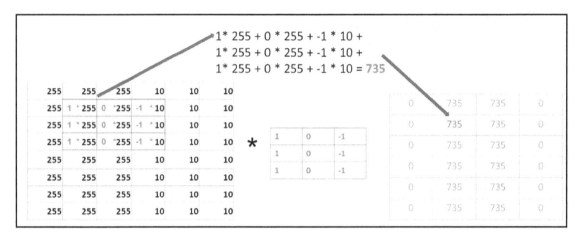

If we were able to continue like this, the output matrix would be exactly like the one on the right side. This is the convolution operation routine. Now, let's look more closely at what happened.

We had the screenshot that was represented by the matrix of numbers, then we convolved with the vertical 3 x 3 filter, and finally, we had the **6 x 4** output matrix:

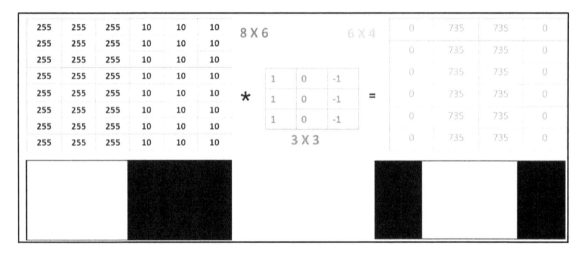

Notice how the pixel dimensions have shrunk a bit. In the next section, we'll look at the impact of reducing the dimensions. Now, if we make the conversion that values greater than **255** are just white, then, using Java, for example, this matrix will be shown as the screenshot in the bottom-right corner. The size would be in black. Now, we are not interested in the size at all, but precisely in the middle, when we expect an edge because the color changes from white to black, we have the white region.

The white region is seen as an edge. It's so wide here because we have really small pixel dimensions of 8 x 6. We'll see another example of this in the next chapter.

Horizontal edge detection

Let's see horizontal edge detection. Here, when compared to vertical edge detection, white depicts up and black depicts down. The edge is supposed to be as shown in the following screenshot:

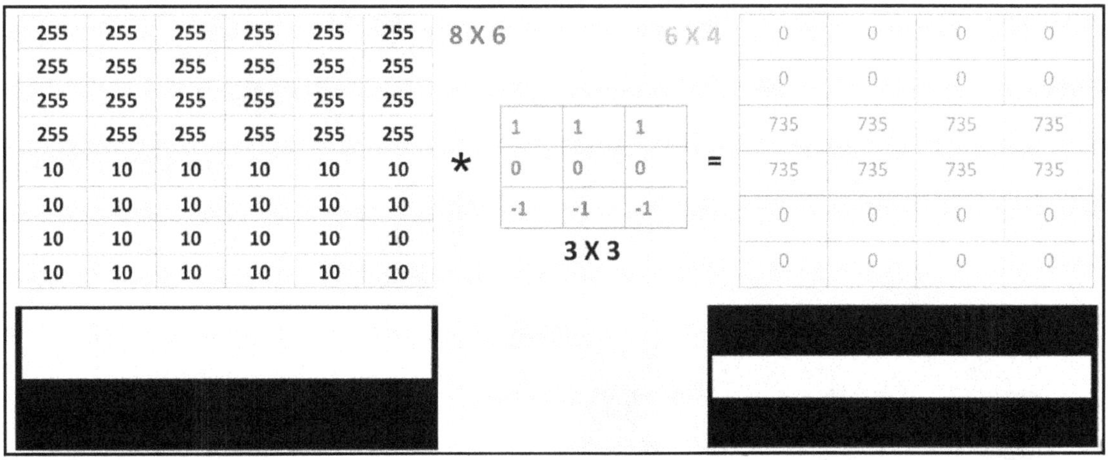

If we were to represent this in the matrix, it would be as shown in the preceding screenshot. As you can see, it's just a flipped version of the vertical filter. The ones that were columns are now rows. The zeros that were the middle column now form the middle row, and the minus one that was the last column is now the last row. This is called a **horizontal filter**. And if we were able to execute the convolution as we saw previously in the routine, we will get this **6×4** matrix. Again, the dimensions have shrunk, and if we were to show this using Java and the conversion we already mentioned, the values greater than **255** are just white, and the sides that we are not interested in are black, but in the middle right away, when we expect the edge, we have the white region. This region is wide because the pixel measures are small, but if we execute it, as we will do in the next chapter, in normal images it should be quite narrow, actually detecting the edge in the white region.

Edge detection intuition

By now, you have an idea of what the edge detection is doing, but let's go back through what's happened so far.

Let's suppose we take the black and white screenshot again, and we have the two filters in different positions: a vertical filter with red, and the horizontal filter with green:

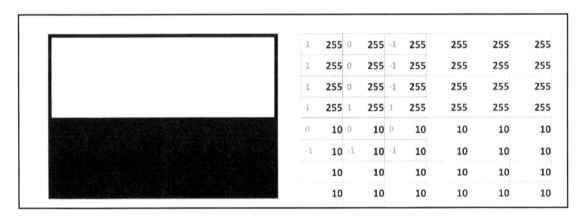

Now, regardless of their position and shape, they have one thing in common: the middle column and the middle row are completely ignored, because of the zeros:

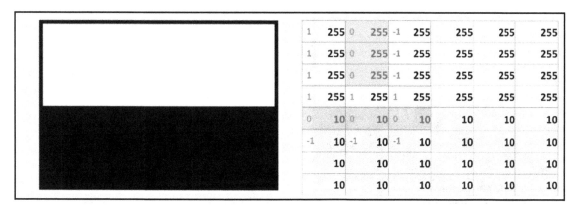

These two filters are only interested in the sides. And depending on these sides' values, we have two states:

When the sides are identical, the difference would be **0**, and this means that we won't have any edge:

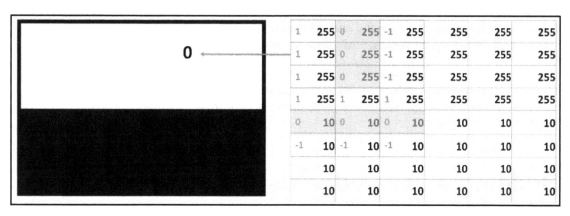

We're just in the middle of the white, or maybe, in the middle of the black, but not near an edge.

If the sides are different, based on the value of the difference, we shall conclude it is an edge. In this case, it will be **735**:

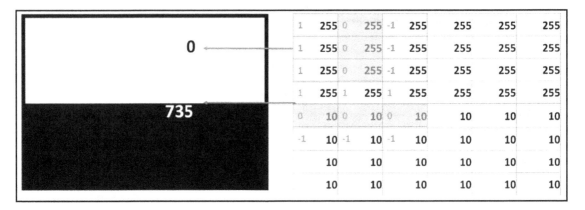

As shown in the preceding screenshot, the place where **735** appears to be, is precisely the edge. This means that a number indicates an edge and 0 indicates no edge, and this is determined by calculating the difference between the sides.

Now, notice how, if we interchange the rows, the terms will be up and **255** will be down; then it will be just minus **735**. But if we were to take the convention of using absolute values, then it's still an edge in the end. The edge detection application we'll see in the next section will use absolute values, and you'll see how it's able to detect all the edges in the images.

This was all about edge detection. Now, we'll run a Java edge detection application using different filters than what we have seen so far, and with more complex images, to see what happens.

Building a Java edge detection application

Now, we'll see different type of filters and apply them to different images. Also, we'll explore how the neural network is using convolution or edge detection.

Types of filters

There are other types of filters apart from the vertical and horizontal filters we've seen so far:

1	0	-1
1	0	-1
1	0	-1

Vertical

1	0	-1
2	0	-2
1	0	-1

Sobel Vertical

3	0	-3
10	0	-10
3	0	-3

Scharr Vertical

1	1	1
0	0	0
-1	-1	-1

Horizontal

Two other popular filters are as follows:

- **Sobel**: This filter simply adds a little bit more weight or value to the middle
- **Scharr**: Besides adding even more weight to the middle, this filter also adds weight to the sides

As we can see, the zeros are placed in the middle column of the Vertical, Sobel, and Scharr filters. Hence, we can say that Sobel and Scharr measure the difference between the left and right side, so, in a way, they're vertical filters.

As you might have already guessed, there are also horizontal versions of these filters:

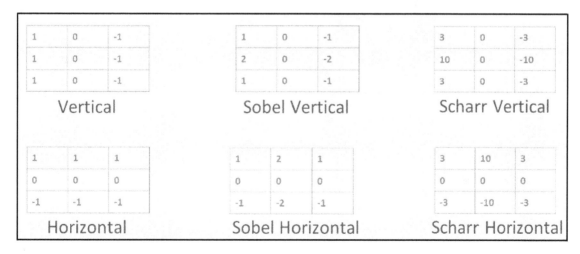

1	0	-1
1	0	-1
1	0	-1

Vertical

1	0	-1
2	0	-2
1	0	-1

Sobel Vertical

3	0	-3
10	0	-10
3	0	-3

Scharr Vertical

1	1	1
0	0	0
-1	-1	-1

Horizontal

1	2	1
0	0	0
-1	-2	-1

Sobel Horizontal

3	10	3
0	0	0
-3	-10	-3

Scharr Horizontal

Horizontal filters are basically a flipped version of the vertical filter. Columns turn to rows. It looks like a right-flipped version, transforming all the columns into rows.

Basic coding

Now, let's have a quick look at the Java code doing the convolution, and then build the Java application with the six filter types we have already seen, along with some different images of course.

This is the main class, `EdgeDetection`:

```
package ramo.klevis.ml;
import javax.imageio.ImageIO;
import java.awt.*;
import java.awt.image.BufferedImage;
import java.io.File;
import java.io.IOException;
import java.util.HashMap;
public class EdgeDetection {
```

We'll start by defining the six filters, with their values, that we saw in the previous section:

```
public static final String HORIZONTAL_FILTER = "Horizontal Filter";
public static final String VERTICAL_FILTER = "Vertical Filter";
public static final String SOBEL_FILTER_VERTICAL = "Sobel Vertical Filter";
public static final String SOBEL_FILTER_HORIZONTAL = "Sobel Horizontal
Filter";
public static final String SCHARR_FILTER_VETICAL = "Scharr Vertical
Filter";
public static final String SCHARR_FILTER_HORIZONTAL = "Scharr Horizontal
Filter";
private static final double[][] FILTER_VERTICAL = {{1, 0, -1}, {1, 0, -1},
{1, 0, -1}};
private static final double[][] FILTER_HORIZONTAL = {{1, 1, 1}, {0, 0, 0},
{-1, -1, -1}};
private static final double[][] FILTER_SOBEL_V = {{1, 0, -1}, {2, 0, -2},
{1, 0, -1}};
private static final double[][] FILTER_SOBEL_H = {{1, 2, 1}, {0, 0, 0},
{-1, -2, -1}};
private static final double[][] FILTER_SCHARR_V = {{3, 0, -3}, {10, 0,
-10}, {3, 0, -3}};
private static final double[][] FILTER_SCHARR_H = {{3, 10, 3}, {0, 0, 0},
{-3, -10, -3}};
```

Let's define our main method, `detectEdges()`:

```
private final HashMap<String, double[][]> filterMap;
public EdgeDetection() {
  filterMap = buildFilterMap();
}
public File detectEdges(BufferedImage bufferedImage, String selectedFilter)
throws IOException {
  double[][][] image = transformImageToArray(bufferedImage);
  double[][] filter = filterMap.get(selectedFilter);
  double[][] convolvedPixels = applyConvolution(bufferedImage.getWidth(),
  bufferedImage.getHeight(), image, filter);
  return createImageFromConvolutionMatrix(bufferedImage, convolvedPixels);
}
```

`detectEdges` is exposed to the graphical user interface, in order to detect edges, and it takes two inputs: the colored image, `bufferedImage`, and the filter selected by the user, `selectedFilter`. It transforms this into a three-dimensional matrix using the `transformImageToArray()` function. We transform it into a three-dimensional matrix because we have an RGB-colored image.

For each of the colors—red, green, and blue—we build a two-dimensional matrix:

```
private double[][][] transformImageToArray(BufferedImage bufferedImage) {
  int width = bufferedImage.getWidth();
  int height = bufferedImage.getHeight();
double[][][] image = new double[3][height][width];
  for (int i = 0; i < height; i++) {
  for (int j = 0; j < width; j++) {
  Color color = new Color(bufferedImage.getRGB(j, i));
  image[0][i][j] = color.getRed();
  image[1][i][j] = color.getGreen();
  image[2][i][j] = color.getBlue();
  }
  }
  return image;
}
```

Sometimes, the third dimension is called a **soul of the channel**, or the **channels**. In this case, we have three channels, but with convolution, we'll see that it's not that uncommon to see quite high numbers of channels.

We're ready to apply the convolution:

```
private double[][] applyConvolution(int width, int height, double[][][]
image, double[][] filter) {
Convolution convolution = new Convolution();
double[][] redConv = convolution.convolutionType2(image[0], height, width,
filter, 3, 3, 1);
double[][] greenConv = convolution.convolutionType2(image[1], height,
width, filter, 3, 3, 1);
double[][] blueConv = convolution.convolutionType2(image[2], height,
width, filter, 3, 3, 1);
double[][] finalConv = new double[redConv.length][redConv[0].length];
for (int i = 0; i < redConv.length; i++) {
for (int j = 0; j < redConv[i].length; j++) {
finalConv[i][j] = redConv[i][j] + greenConv[i][j] + blueConv[i][j];
}
}
return finalConv;
}
```

Notice that we're applying a convolution separately for each of the basic colors:

- With `convolution.convolutionType2(image[0], height, width, filter, 3, 3, 1);`, we apply the two-dimensional matrix of red
- With `convolution.convolutionType2(image[1], height, width, filter, 3, 3, 1);`, we apply the two-dimensional matrix of green
- With `convolution.convolutionType2(image[2], height, width, filter, 3, 3, 1);`, we apply the two-dimensional matrix of blue

Then, with `double[][]`, we get back three two-dimensional matrices of the three colors, which means they are convolved. The final convolved matrix, `double[][] finalConv`, will be the addition of `redConv[i][j] + greenConv[i][j] + blueConv[i][j];`. We'll go into more detail when we build the application, but for now, the reason why we add this together is because we aren't interested in a color any more, or not in the original form at least, but we *are* interested in the edge. So, as we will see, in the output image, the high-level features such as the edge, will be black and white because we are adding the three color convolutions together.

Now we have `double[][] convolvedPixels`, the two-dimensional convolved pixels defined in `detectEdges()`, and we need to show it in `createImageFromConvolutionMatrix()`:

```
  private File createImageFromConvolutionMatrix(BufferedImage originalImage,
  double[][] imageRGB) throws IOException {
  BufferedImage writeBackImage = new BufferedImage(originalImage.getWidth(),
  originalImage.getHeight(), BufferedImage.TYPE_INT_RGB);
  for (int i = 0; i < imageRGB.length; i++) {
  for (int j = 0; j < imageRGB[i].length; j++) {
  Color color = new Color(fixOutOfRangeRGBValues(imageRGB[i][j]),
  fixOutOfRangeRGBValues(imageRGB[i][j]),
  fixOutOfRangeRGBValues(imageRGB[i][j]));
  writeBackImage.setRGB(j, i, color.getRGB());
  }
  }

        File outputFile = new File("EdgeDetection/edgesTmp.png");
        ImageIO.write(writeBackImage, "png", outputFile);
        return outputFile;
    }
```

First, we need to transform these pixels into an image. We do that using `fixOutOfRangeRGBValues(imageRGB[i][j])`, `fixOutOfRangeRGBValues(imageRGB[i][j]));`.

The only thing we want to see right now is the method, `fixOutOfRangeRGBValues`:

```
  private int fixOutOfRangeRGBValues(double value) {
  if (value < 0.0) {
  value = -value;
  }
  if (value > 255) {
  return 255;
  } else {
  return (int) value;
  }
  }
```

This takes the absolute value of the pixel, because, as we saw, sometimes we have negative values when the difference isn't from black to white, but actually from white to black. For us, it's not important since we want to detect only the edges, so we take the absolute value, with values that are greater than 255, as just 255 as the maximum, since Java and other similar languages, such as C#, can't handle more than 255 in the RGB format. We simply write it as edge, `.png` file `EdgeDetection/edgesTmp.png`.

Now, let's see this application with a number of samples.

Let's try a horizontal filter:

This edge is quite narrow this image has sufficient pixels:

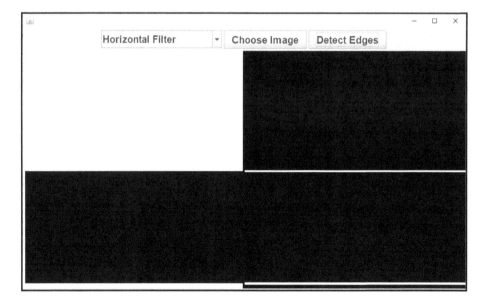

Let's try with the **Vertical Filter**, which gives us that looks like an edge:

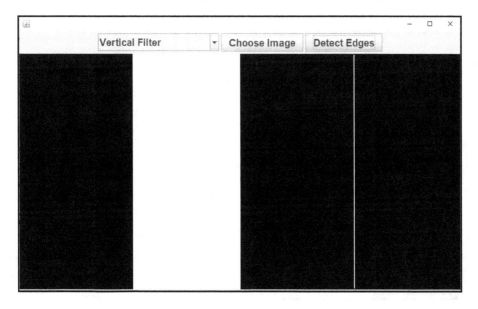

Let's try a **Vertical Filter** on a more complex image. As you can see in the following screenshot, all the vertical lines are detected:

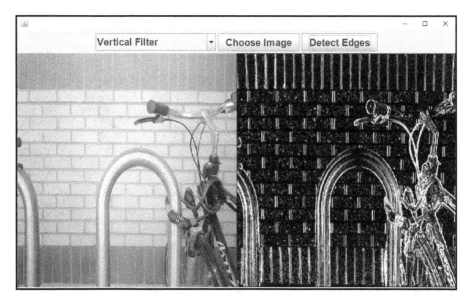

Now, let's see the same image with a **Horizontal Filter**:

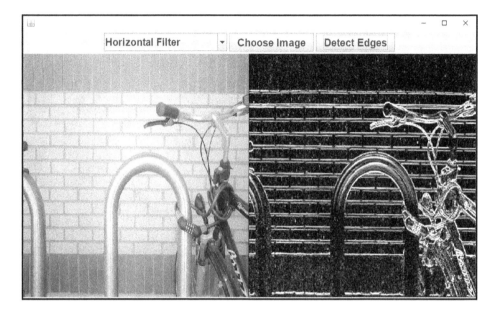

The horizontal filter didn't detect any of the vertical edges, but it actually detected the horizontal ones.

Let's see what the **Sobel Horizontal Filter** does:

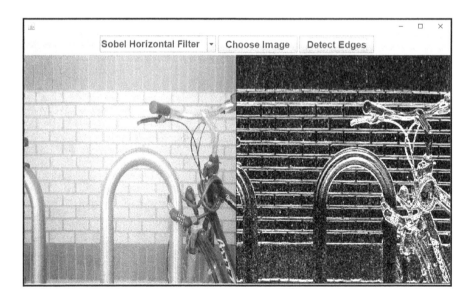

It simply added a bit more light, and this is because adding more weight means you make these edges a bit wider.

Let's now look at the **Sobel Vertical Filter**:

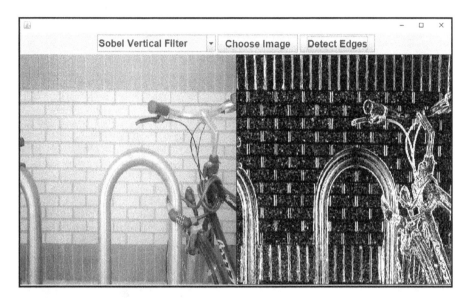

Again, this should be brighter.

And here's the **Scharr Vertical Filter**:

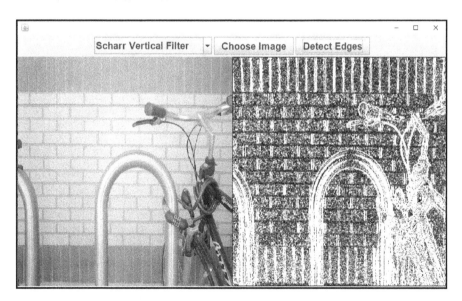

Not surprisingly, the **Scharr Vertical Filter** adds more weight, so we see more bright edges. The edges are wider and are more sensitive to the color changes from one side to the other—the horizontal filter wouldn't be any different.

In our color image, of a butterfly, the horizontal filter will be something like this:

Let's see the **Sobel Horizontal Filter**:

It's a bit brighter.

And let's see what the equivalent **Scharr Horizontal Filter** does:

It's also quite a bit brighter.

Let's also try the **Scharr Vertical Filter**:

Feel free to try it on your own images, because it won't be strange if you find a filter that actually performs better—sometimes, the results of the filters depend on the images.

The question now is how to find the best filter for our neural network. Is it the Sobel one, or maybe the Scharr, which is sensitive to the changes, or maybe a very simple filter, such as the vertical or horizontal one?

The answer, of course, isn't straightforward, and, as we mentioned, it depends partly on the images, their color, and low levels. So why don't we just let the neural network choose the filter? Aren't the neural networks the best at predicting things? The neural network will have to learn which filter is the best for the problem it's trying to predict.

Basically, the neural network will learn the classical ways we saw in the hidden layers of the neurons—in the dense layers. This will be exactly the same, just the operation is not the simple multiplication operation; it will be convolution multiplication. But these are just normal weights that the neural network has to learn:

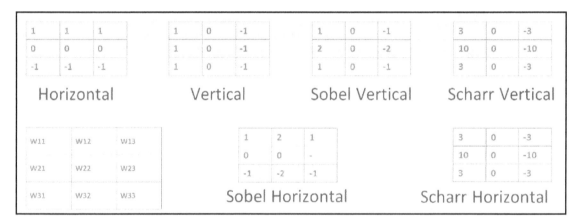

Instead of giving the values, allow the neural network to work to find these weights.

This is a fundamental concept that enables deep neural networks to detect more specialized features, such as edge detection, and even more high-level features, such as eyes, the wheels of cars, and faces. And we'll see that the deeper you go with convolution layers, the more high-level features you detect.

Convolution on RGB images

Let's see how convolution is done with color images, and how we can obtain multi-dimensional output matrices.

As we saw previously, a color image is represented as a three-dimensional matrix of numbers:

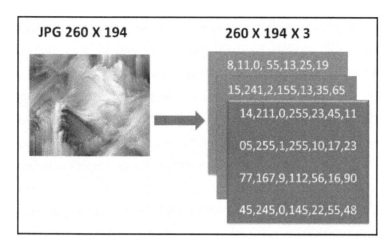

The third dimension is usually called **all the channels**. In this case, we have three channels: red, green, and blue. Considering how the convolution was done with the grayscale images, just convolving a two-dimensional matrix with one filter, one reasonable thing to do here—since we have three of the two-dimensional matrices—is to convolve with three filters:

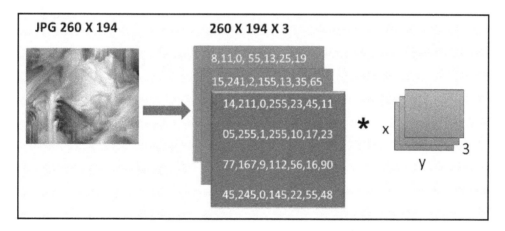

Each of these filters will be convolved with one of the channels.

So far, we've seen 3 x 3 filters, but actually, the two dimensions can vary from x to ε.

This kind of operation will now produce three outputs:

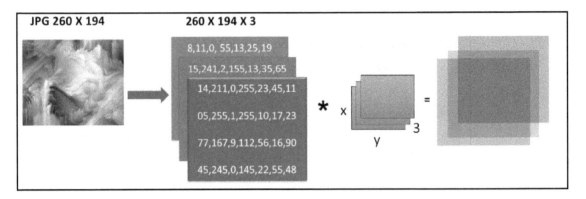

Let's look in a bit more detail at what's happened so far.

Let's take the following example:

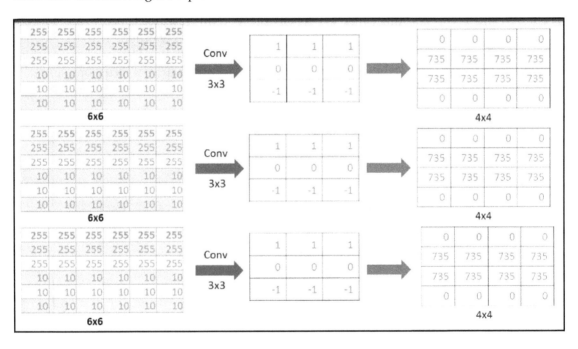

We have three **6 x 6** images that represent the channels, and they will be convolved with three **3 x 3** filters, and, in the end, we'll have three **4 x 4** outputs. Notice now how these three 4 x 4 matrices don't represent the same pixel values as in the input.

So the question here really is: *Does it make sense to keep them separated, since these matrices now are detecting edges rather than colors, or are these the same channels?* Indeed, many experiments have shown that keeping them separate doesn't add any value besides wasting resources. Hence, one reasonable thing to do here is to add them together:

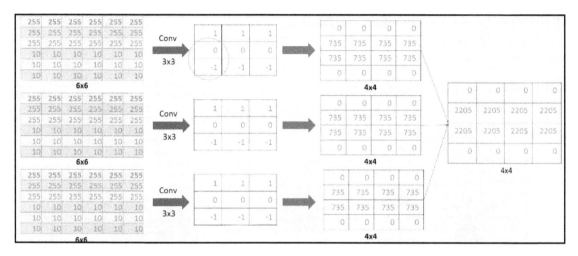

In the end, we'll have just one **4 x 4** matrix, so each of these cells will be added. These values are uniform at the moment, just to make it simple, but, in reality, they will vary a lot.

To summarize once again:

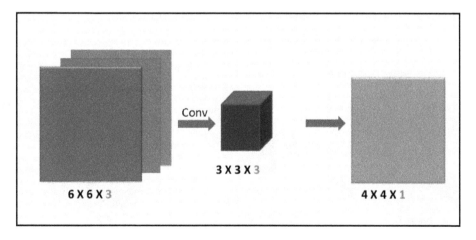

We had a 6 x 6 three-input image, which will convolve with three 3 x 3 filters, and since the convolution product will be summed in the end, we have just one two-dimensional matrix, 4 x 4. So, with the convolution, the number of channels—regardless of the input—will be always reduced to 1; in this case, from 3 to 1. And notice how the two-dimensional matrix will shrink from 6 to 4. Usually in convolution architectures, it's OK to reduce the two dimensions, but, on the other hand, we require a large number of channels. We want a greater number of channels because we want to be able to detect more features, or to capture more features.

For example, we may want not one channel but five:

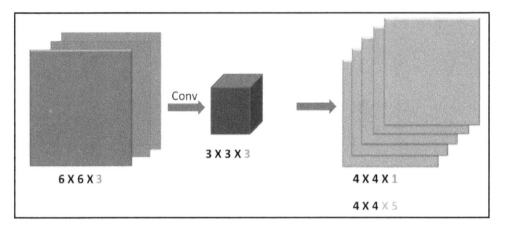

One way to solve this simply is just to add five 3 x 3 x 3 filters:

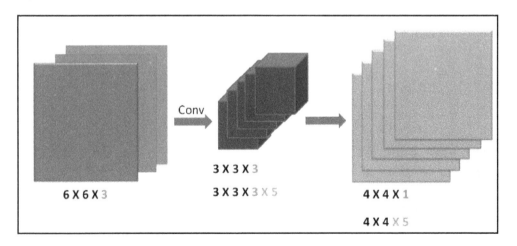

In this case, for example, let's suppose the filter in the image is the horizontal filter, and so inside this, we'll have three horizontal filters convolving with three channels. Since we'll sum in the end, this will give just the 4 x 4 two-dimensional matrix. Then, if this is a vertical filter, convolving and summing will give a 4 x 4 two-dimensional matrix, and if we consider the filter as a Sobel, or maybe a Scharr, maybe the output would come up as in our previous experiments. Each of these filters will give a different two-dimensional matrix.

We can even go one step further and convolve with a **3 x 3 x 5** filter:

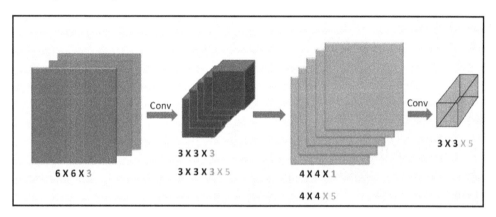

Since the five filters will be convolved separately with each of the input channels, and in the end they'll sum, we'll gain a **2 x 2 x 1** two-dimensional matrix:

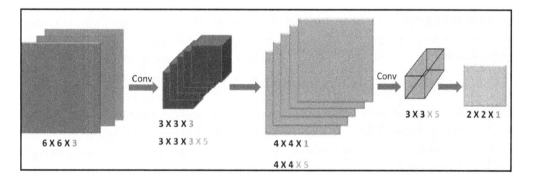

If we want to increase the filters to three, we'll just add three **3 x 3 x 5** filters:

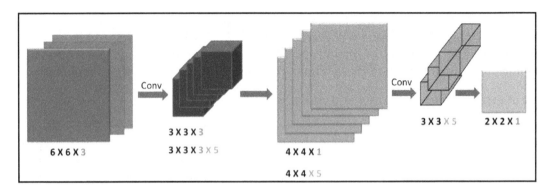

Notice how the third dimension of the filters is always equal to the third dimension of the input. It's always equal because we need five filters to handle the five input channels, and, in the end of course, that will produce just one, because of the final sum, but again we need five of them to handle the five channels.

We'll now see how to control the output matrix dimensions by introducing a number of parameters and techniques.

Working with convolutional layers' parameters

We'll see how to increase the dimension of the output matrix by using padding, and how to greatly decrease it through use of the stride. You will recall from the previous section, that we're convolving a **6 x 6 x 3** input image with **3 x 3** filters, which gives us a **4 x 4 x 1** matrix output:

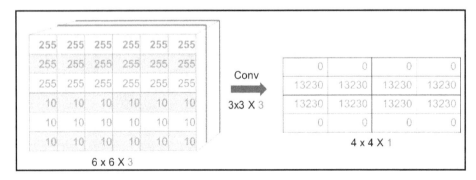

And as you may have guessed, these output dimensions can be described by a math formula, and that formula appears as follows:

$$OM = IM - F + 1$$

In this equation, IM is just the input matrix dimension, OM is the output matrix dimension, and F refers to the filter size. So let's apply this formula:

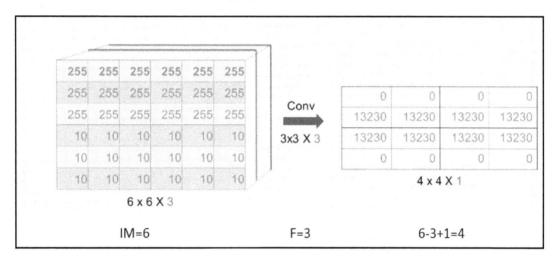

We can do the same for the other dimension as well. Feel free to try a different size of input images with different filters, and see how this formula will actually work. You can do that even for the edge detection application. Regardless of this formula, we have shrunk the dimensions from 6 to 4, and that will always be the case if we use this technique and formula. But what if we want to increase the output dimension from 4? Here's where padding helps.

Padding

One way to maybe increase the dimensions to 4 x 4 would be to introduce padding.

Padding by 1, for example, just adds one full rectangle of zeros, as shown in the following screenshot:

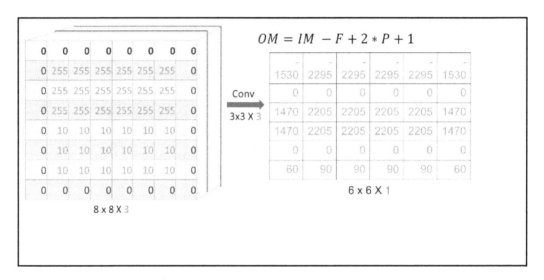

And by doing that, we increase the dimension of the input images from 6 to 8, so now we have **8 x 8 x 3**, and by applying the formula we'll have, for example, *8-3+1=6*. Now, notice how it was increased from 4 x 4 to 6 x 6; the 6 x 6 of the output is equal to the original input image, which is the blue color in the input matrix. In the literature, this phenomenon is called the **Same Convolution**, so the same convolution refers to the fact that the output convolve matrix has the same dimensions as the original input image.

Now, to be 100% correct here, we need to fix a bit of this formula, because the input matrix dimensions are not 8 but 6. In order to introduce the padding, we'll add this term:

$$OM = IM - F + 2 * P + 1 + 2 * P$$

Here, *2*P* is the padding. Let's try this new formula now:

$$6 - 3 + 1 + 2 \times 1 = 6 \times 1$$

We've learned how to increase the dimensions, although the convolution, by default, will decrease if we don't do anything like padding. There could be cases when we want to increase even more, and one way to do that is by introducing stride.

Stride

Stride just increases the step size of this convolution window, which we saw previously:

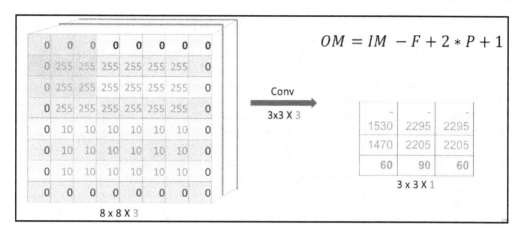

Instead of going one step, we can go two steps, as follows:

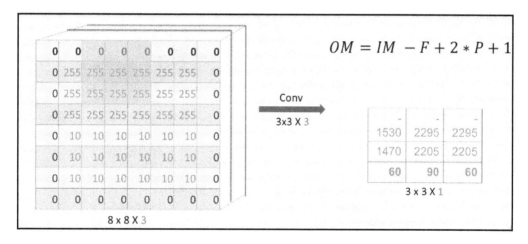

And we do the same thing each time until we reach the position in the bottom-right corner. Notice how the dimension of the output matrix was shrunk to 3 x 3 x 1, and if we increase the stride again, we may end up even with a smaller matrix. This formula has now changed a bit, so we just divide it by the stride:

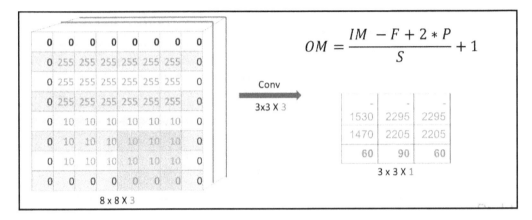

This division actually shows that the stride can dramatically decrease the dimension numbers of the matrix. Let's try to apply this formula once again:

IM=6, *F=3*, stride *S=2*:

$$\frac{6 - 3 + 2 \times 1}{2} = 2.5$$

But we take the 2 and have this as the formula:

$$2 + 1 = 3$$

Basically that's it for padding and stride, and these two operations actually give us a lot of flexibility. We can play with these three parameters, and from there we can have what we want, which as an output matrix dimension, rather than getting the default behavior of the convolution, which is reduced by the first formula we already saw.

We're now ready to learn about a new layer, called the **pooling layers**; although they're similar to the convolution layer, they introduce a slightly different operation and also have different characteristics.

Pooling layers

Let's see a slightly different type of layer, pooling layers, and, more specifically, we'll go in to the details of max pooling and average pooling.

Max pooling

Let's first explore how max pooling works. Similar to the convolution, we have the same parameters, the filter size is 2 x 2, the stride defines how big the step is, and we won't use any padding here:

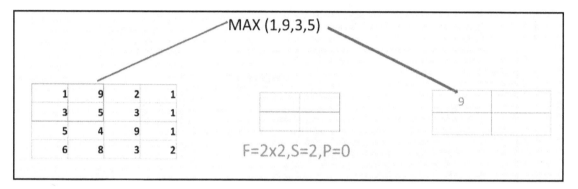

Max pooling simply outputs the maximum of the selected values from the filter window, and, in this case, it would be nine.

It then moves the window on the right:

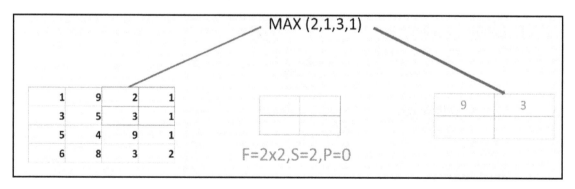

In this case, it moves two steps because of the stride, and outputs the maximum of the selected values, which is three.

It then moves down two steps and it outputs eight:

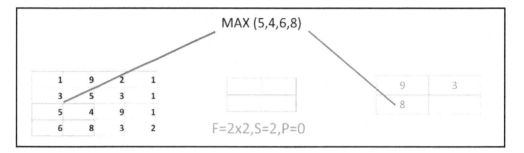

In this case, and in the next step on the right, it will output nine, because this is the maximum value of these selected values:

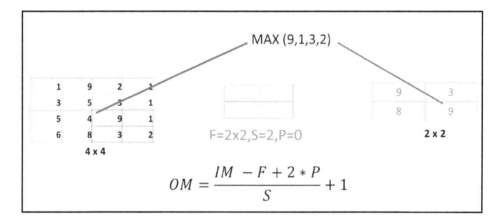

And, as we can see, the input matrix has a 4 x 4 dimension, while the output is 2 x 2. The formula from the previous section on convolution also works in relation to the max pool:

$$\frac{4 - 2 + 2 \times 0}{2} = 1$$

We also have the following:

$$1 + 1 = 2$$

So, basically, the formula we saw in the convolution works perfectly here, which means that we have three parameters to play with, that is, to control the output matrix dimensions. Let's now look at average pooling.

Average pooling

Nowadays, average pooling is used very rarely, because max pooling will usually outperform average pooling. But anyway let's see what average pooling is doing, which isn't that different from max pooling.

Again, it has the same parameters—the filter size, stride, and padding 0151 but instead of outputting the maximum of the selected values, it outputs their average:

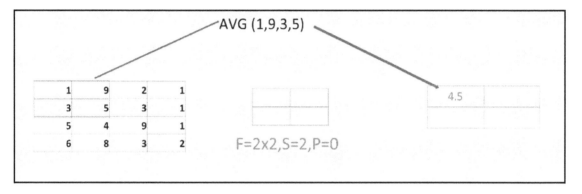

In this case, the average of these values will be **4.5**, and, when we move two steps and repeat this, we will finally get the following:

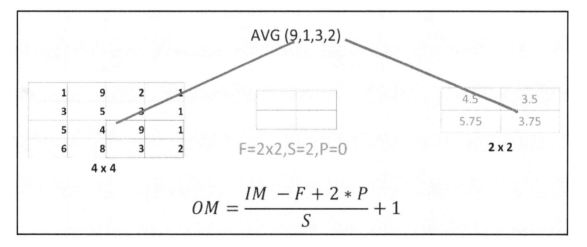

$$OM = \frac{IM - F + 2 * P}{S} + 1$$

The formula we saw for max pooling, which was borrowed from a convolution formula, also works perfectly for average pooling, so these three parameters can be used to control the output dimensions as we want.

Pooling on RGB images

So far, we've seen the pooling layer operations, max and average pooling, with a two-dimensional matrix. But, as we saw, RGB images and color images are three-dimensional matrices, with three channels, so the value of the third dimension is three:

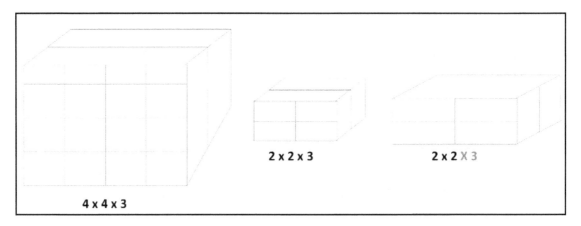

Similar to the convolution, we'll also take three filters, and for each of the filters we'll do the operation we saw in the previous section independently. The filter will handle the pooling layer operation with the channel. It will, of course, produce three two-dimensional matrices, which will be the product of the three independent operations.

Now, if you recall from the convolution, because those matrices were no longer presenting colors, we added those matrices together, and therefore had only one matrix in the end. Well, this final step won't be done in the pooling layers. The pooling layers aren't adding those matrices together, but leaving them as they are.

So, the third dimension was 3, and with max pooling, for example, the output will also be 3. The third dimension is left untouched. If it were a convolution layer, we'd still have three filters, but the third dimension would be cut to 1.

Pooling characteristics

To summarize once again, the pooling layers always leave the third dimension untouched. We usually misunderstand this with a convolution which reduced 1, but that is not happening with max pooling. Usually pooling layers are used to reduce the first two dimensions because it's quite common to use the stride with them, and they usually do a good job of reducing overfitting.

As you will recall from the convolution, we don't specify the nature of the feature to use. We don't tell the neural network to use vertical, horizontal, Sobel, or Scharr filter; instead, we let the neural network figure out what filter is best for the job it's trying to solve. And this means that the values of the filters are just some parameters to be learned by the neural network.

Well, as regards max pooling, there's no parameter to be learned, it's just a transformation of the input matrix to the output matrix. So, one of the questions with max pooling or average pooling is as follows: *What's the idea behind them? What are they doing that offers such good results?* Well this question is very hard to answer, and use of the pooling layers is mostly based on the experiment results, which show great improvements after using them. But the best thing in my personal opinions is that, they're trying to capture dominant features or dominant activation's from previous layers.

For example, with a nine value, we saw previously that if the nine value will be another part of the image, max pooling will actually preserve that value and use it as an input for the next layer. Somehow, the maximum activation survived on the next layer, and those that are smaller actually kind of cut off. But again, this idea may not work for you and that's OK. It is usually very difficult to explain in literature what they do so well.

Are you excited about using all the building blocks you've learned so far to build a working neural network architecture?

Building and training a Convolution Neural Network

So far, we've examined all the building blocks needed to build a **Convolutional Neural Network (CNN)**, and that's exactly what we are going to do in this section, where we explain why convolution is so efficient and widely used.

Here's the architecture of a CNN:

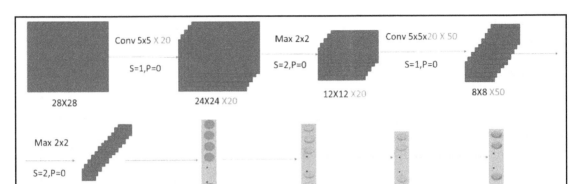

First, we start with a **28 x 28** grayscale image, so we have one channel that's just a black-and-white image. For now, it doesn't really matter, but these are handwritten digit images taken from the MNIST dataset that we saw in the previous chapter.

In the first layer, we'll apply a 5 x 5 filter, a convolution feed filter, with a stride of 1 and no padding, and, applying the formula we saw in the previous section will give us a 24 x 24 output matrix. But since we want a higher number of channels, in order to capture more features, we will apply 20 of these filters, and that gives us the final output of **24 x 24 x 20**. So we have a 24 x 24 matrix. In the next layer, we'll apply a max pooling of 2 x 2, a stride of 2, and no padding. That basically shrinks the first two dimensions' widths by dividing by 2, so we'll have 12 x 12, and max pooling leaves the third dimension untouched, so we'll have 20 as the number of channels at the input.

In the next layer, we'll apply a convolution of 5 x 5, again with a stride of 1 and no padding. Since the input now has 20 channels, we have to have 20 of these 5 x 5 filters. So each of these filters will be convolved separately with each of these 20 channels and, in the end, the product will be totaled to give just one matrix: 8 x 8. But again, since we want a higher number of channels, in this case 50, we need to apply 50 structures of **5 x 5 x 20**.

So, in a few words: convolving **5 x 5 x 20** with **12 x 12 x 20** will give us just one matrix, and having 50 such filters will give us **8 x 8 x 50**.

In the fourth layer, and in the last convolution layer, we'll have max pooling again, 2 x 2, a stride of 2, and no padding. That divides the first dimensions by 2 and leaves the number of channels untouched. At the fourth layer, the convolution part is finished.

Now, we're going to use a simple neural network, full of connected hidden layers, that we've already seen. The output of the convolution will be transformed to a one-dimensional vector, with 800 inputs; there are 800 because that's simply the result of **4 x 4 x 50**. Each of these 800 inputs will be fully connected with the first dense layer or the hidden layer, which will have 128 neurons, and then the activation's of these 128 neurons will be fully connected with the second hidden layer of 64 neurons. Then, through a softmax, we'll have 10 different classes, each representing digits, the prediction of digits from 0 to 9. And, as we'll see, this modified architecture will give us a much higher accuracy – more than 99%, instead of the 97% that we were stuck at.

Why convolution?

So why is convolution so efficient? In order to see that, let's suppose for a moment that we are not using the convolution layer, but instead, a fully-connected or dense layer:

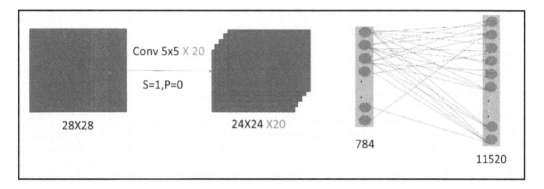

So, we have the input, 784, which is just a multiplication of **28 x 28**, and the first hidden layer or dense layer, which is **11,520**. Basically, multiplying the multiplication of the three numbers will give **11,520**.

Since this is fully-connected, which means that each of the input, is connected to all of the outputs, it means that for each input, we have 11,500 parameters to learn. In total, that's 9,000,000 parameters to learn. Imagine this is just the first hidden layer; usually neuron networks have many of these hidden layers. Hence, basically, this doesn't look that promising.

As we know, when we use convolution, we don't predefine the nature of the filter, so we don't say it's a Sobel, horizontal, or vertical, but we rather let the neural network figure out the type of filter it wants to learn. And that means that the cells in the filters are just parameters. And the number of cells on this filter, if the image is **5 x 5 x 20**, gives us 500 parameters. So we are comparing 500 parameters versus 9,000,000 parameters.

This is what we gain using convolution: we have fewer parameters, but, at the same time, the neural network's ability to predict is retained. Adding more dense layers will sometimes just slow it down and not provide any good performance. Although this is the best way to demonstrate as to why convolution is so efficient, there are two other ways of seeing that, and one of them is parameter sharing.

Parameter-sharing says that the filter that works on one position will also work just fine on the other positions:

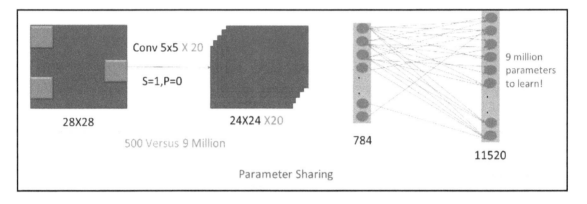

Parameter Sharing

So basically, you don't need three other filters; one type of filter on one position, another type of filter on another position, and the other one on another position. What works at one position will also work at other positions. And that, as you can imagine, reduces the number of parameters dramatically.

Similarly, we have the sparsity of the connections. The sparsity of the connections says that only a small part of the image or matrix is connected to the filter, and basically only these pixels under the selected window are connected, and the other pixels are just isolated, so they aren't connected at all, and that means that you have fewer parameters. The parameters you have to learn are only those connected with the filter at one time.

Another idea is that convolution makes the neural network prediction more robust, so a cat that is a little bit on the right, or on the left, or maybe skewed up and down, is just a cat for a convolution neural network.

We'll now apply the architecture to build a Java application for handwritten digits, and we'll get a much higher occurrence doing that.

Improving the handwritten digit recognition application

Let's see how our CNN architecture will look when written in Java. We'll also run the Java application and test the improved model from the graphical user interface. We'll draw some digits and ask models for predictions, and maybe simulate a case when a convolution will outperform the simple neural network model.

Before checking out the code, let's first look at the CNN architecture that we saw in the previous section from a different point of view:

	Activation Matrix (Input)	Activation Size	Parameters Size
Image Matrix	28 X 28 X 1	784	0
Conv 5X5X20,S=1	24 X 24 X 20	11520	500
Max 2 X 2 S=2	12 X 12 X 20	2880	0
Conv 5X5X50,S=1	8 X 8 X 50	3200	1250
Max 2 X 2 S=2	4 X 4 X 50	800	0
FC1	128 X 1	128	102400
FC2	64 X 1	64	8192
OUT	10 X 1	10	640

So, we have this table here, and in the extreme left, there are the layers. Then we have these two columns, which are the activation's. So the activations are just the input, hidden layers, or convolution layers, and one activation shows the shape of the matrix dimensions, while the other shows the complete size, which is just a multiplication of the values in the first activation. The parameters are the connection between the input or the activation's, so they're the activation's in the previous layer with the output in the next layer. And we can see that the activation's decrease from layer to layer until we get the output size of 10, while the parameters more or less increase over time. We have the zeros because for max pooling, there's nothing to learn, and since we've just started, we can't learn anything. Over time, we'll see an increase, and even after the convolution, we'll see a dramatic increase in the parameters; as we have already seen, the fully connected layers explore the parameters to learn.

Now, let's jump into the code. As always, let's start with some parameters:

```java
public class DigitRecognizerConvolutionalNeuralNetwork {
private static final String OUT_DIR =
"HandWrittenDigitRecognizer/src/main/resources/cnnCurrentTrainingModels";
 private static final String TRAINED_MODEL_FILE =
"HandWrittenDigitRecognizer/src/main/resources/cnnTrainedModels/bestModel.b
in";
 private MultiLayerNetwork preTrainedModel;
private static final int CHANNELS = 1;
 /**
 * Number prediction classes.
 * We have 0-9 digits so 10 classes in total.
 */
 private static final int OUTPUT = 10;
 /**
 * Mini batch gradient descent size or number of matrices processed in
parallel.
 * For CORE-I7 16 is good for GPU please change to 128 and up
 */
 private static final int MINI_BATCH_SIZE = 16;// Number of training epochs
 /**
 * Number of total traverses through data. In this case it is used as the
maximum epochs we allow
 * with 5 epochs we will have 5/@MINI_BATCH_SIZE iterations or weights
updates
 */
 private static final int MAX_EPOCHS = 20;
/**
 * The alpha learning rate defining the size of step towards the minimum
 */
private static final double LEARNING_RATE = 0.01;
/**
 * https://en.wikipedia.org/wiki/Random_seed
 */
 private static final int SEED = 123;
```

We specify the number of channels by `private static final int OUTPUT` which is 10, so we have digits 0 to 9 for prediction classes, the mini burst size specified by `private static final int MINI_BATCH_SIZE` is the level of parallelism; which is 16 because we are using a CPU, but for GPU, feel free to increase this value. By epoch in, `MAX_EPOCHS` we mean, maximum number of iteration through the data.

Having these parameters in place, we are now ready to build the architecture.

First, we define the parameters:

```
MultiLayerConfiguration conf = new NeuralNetConfiguration.Builder()
 .seed(SEED)
 .learningRate(LEARNING_RATE)
 .weightInit(WeightInit.XAVIER)
 .optimizationAlgo(OptimizationAlgorithm.STOCHASTIC_GRADIENT_DESCENT)
 .updater(Updater.NESTEROVS)
 .list()
 .layer(0, new ConvolutionLayer.Builder(5, 5)
 .nIn(CHANNELS)
 .stride(1, 1)
 .nOut(20)
 .activation(Activation.IDENTITY)
 .build())
 .layer(1, new SubsamplingLayer.Builder(SubsamplingLayer.PoolingType.MAX)
 .kernelSize(2, 2)
 .stride(2, 2)
 .build())
 .layer(2, new ConvolutionLayer.Builder(5, 5)
 .nIn(20)
 .stride(1, 1)
 .nOut(50)
 .activation(Activation.IDENTITY)
 .build())
 .layer(3, new SubsamplingLayer.Builder(SubsamplingLayer.PoolingType.MAX)
 .kernelSize(2, 2)
 .stride(2, 2)
 .build())
 .layer(4, new DenseLayer.Builder().activation(Activation.RELU)
 .nIn(800)
 .nOut(128).build())
 .layer(5, new DenseLayer.Builder().activation(Activation.RELU)
 .nIn(128)
 .nOut(64).build())
 .layer(6, new
OutputLayer.Builder(LossFunctions.LossFunction.NEGATIVELOGLIKELIHOOD)
 .nOut(OUTPUT)
 .activation(Activation.SOFTMAX)
 .build())
 .setInputType(InputType.convolutionalFlat(28, 28, 1))
 .backprop(true).pretrain(false).build();
EarlyStoppingConfiguration earlyStoppingConfiguration = new
EarlyStoppingConfiguration.Builder()
 .epochTerminationConditions(new MaxEpochsTerminationCondition(MAX_EPOCHS))
 .scoreCalculator(new AccuracyCalculator(new
```

```
MnistDataSetIterator(MINI_BATCH_SIZE, false, 12345)))
  .evaluateEveryNEpochs(1)
  .modelSaver(new LocalFileModelSaver(OUT_DIR))
  .build();
```

Things such as weight initialization, `WeightInit`, which is `xavier`, helps us to start. Then, we use the exponentially-weighted average updater, or the momentum updater, and then we move to the first convolution layer, which is just a 5 x 5 filter with a stride of one. We have two ones in `.Strides(1,1)` because it's possible to use a different stride for right and for down, but we use one for both of them. Now, notice that we aren't defining the first two dimensions.

When using Deeplearning4j, the first two dimensions are somehow figured out, but you need to define only the channels, which is the third dimension of the matrix. And we start with one channel for black and white, and then we have 20, so, `nOut(20)` means we have the 5 x 5 x 20 layer, which has been shown in the architecture. We then move to the max pooling layer, which is defined as `.kernelSize(2,2)` and `.Stride(2,2)`. We don't need to define any input and output because the max pooling layer doesn't change the number of channels, and the first two dimensions are already defined.

Then, we have the other convolution layer, 5 x 5, the number of the input channel is 20, and the output is 50, so we increase the number of channels. Then, we have the other max pooling layer, 2 x 2 and a stride of two. That's it for the convolution part. Now begins the part that we've already seen, the dense layer or the fully-connected hidden layers. The number of inputs is 800, so `.nIn(800)`, the number of outputs is 128, `.nout(128)`, so this is the number of neurons in the first fully-connected hidden layer, and we use a ReLU activation, which is the default choice nowadays. Then we have the second hidden layer, which has an input of 128, but 64 new rows as an output. Then, gain, we use the ReLU activation. In the end, we close with the output layer, which is a `softmax` with 10 digits - 0-9. And `.setInputType(InputType.convolutionalFlat(28, 28, 1))` is how Deeplearning4j understands the first two dimensions, because, as we said at the beginning, the shape of the input is 28 x 28, and it only requires the number of channels, which is 1, and then it calculates all the first two dimensions.

The number of inputs isn't required, but in this example, we defined it for the sake of clarity; maybe in other examples we'll omit it.

For training, we use a slightly different technique, called **early stopping**:

```
EarlyStoppingTrainer trainer = new
EarlyStoppingTrainer(earlyStoppingConfiguration, conf, mnistTrain);
EarlyStoppingResult<MultiLayerNetwork> result = trainer.fit();
log.info("Termination reason: " + result.getTerminationReason());
 log.info("Termination details: " + result.getTerminationDetails());
 log.info("Total epochs: " + result.getTotalEpochs());
 log.info("Best epoch number: " + result.getBestModelEpoch());
 log.info("Score at best epoch: " + result.getBestModelScore());
 }
```

As soon as you define a goal, and that goal is accomplished, early stopping immediately stops and gives you the best model seen so far. In our case the goal is simple - we'll say stop as soon as you reach these 20 epochs.

Early stopping requires an evaluator. We use a simple one that takes the test dataset and then evaluates the current model in one of the epochs against this test dataset, and basically takes the model that has the highest accuracy:

```
public class AccuracyCalculator implements
ScoreCalculator<MultiLayerNetwork> {
 private final MnistDataSetIterator dataSetIterator;
 public AccuracyCalculator(MnistDataSetIterator dataSetIterator) {
  this.dataSetIterator = dataSetIterator;
 }
private int i = 0;
@Override
 public double calculateScore(MultiLayerNetwork network) {
 Evaluation evaluate = network.evaluate(dataSetIterator);
 double accuracy = evaluate.accuracy();
 log.info("Accuracy at iteration" + i++ + " " + accuracy);
 return 1 - evaluate.accuracy();
 }
}
```

So, through epochs, it evaluates against the test dataset and saves the model on that epoch that performs best. Then, we analyse every epoch, and, in the end, we save the best model, in other words, the one with the highest accuracy, to this directory. Then we have a matrix that justifies why the early stopping was executed.

Now, let's run the application. It takes a couple of hours to gain good results on 99 or something. Let's see a log I ran for 40 minutes:

It started at 96%, then moved slowly to 98.65%, then to 98.98%, and finally to 99%:

The good thing about the convolution is the more time you give it, the more it improves, while with standard neural networks, even if you leave it for longer, they get stuck at 97%. So the convolution really helps to detect more features and to gain higher accuracy.

Now, let's see the application from the graphical user interface. So let's try with the first digit, a **3**:

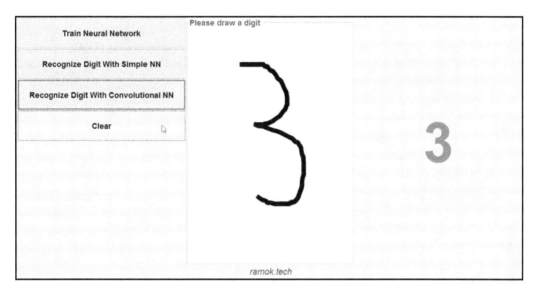

Let's see with a **6**:

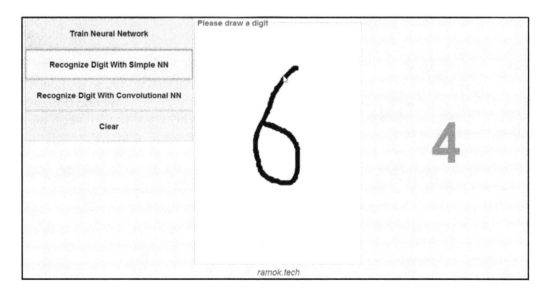

The simple neural networks says **4**, while the CNN is able to detect it:

Similarly, with a 9, the simple neural network says 7, while the CNN says 9. This shows that the CNN does a better job.

Summary

We hope you enjoyed learning about edge detection, and creating an application to detect the edges of complex images using different types of filters. We took an in-depth look at convolution and worked with its layers, which helped us to understand complex convolution neural networks. We saw the benefit of pooling layers in building a CNNs—they reduce the number of parameters drastically. We saw why convolution is the ultimate technique for achieving better accuracy and proved it by building and training a CNN that showed how the accuracy percentage was improving consistently over time rather than sticking at 97%, as with the simple neural networks.

In the next chapter, we'll look at transfer learning and the deep convolution neural network architecture, which will enable us to achieve state-of-the-art accuracy.

3
Transfer Learning and Deep CNN Architectures

In this chapter, we'll discuss the classical **convolutional neural networks** (CNN) that greatly influence computer vision. We will present two advanced architectures: the residual neural network, which solves the problem of training deep neural networks, and the inception network, or GoogLeNet, which dramatically improves computation efficiency through the use of one-by-one convolution.

Next up, we'll gain insights into transfer learning and explore several ways to use it to train neural networks efficiently. Finally, we'll use transfer learning techniques and the VGG-16 architecture to build an animal recognizer Java application and run it through a graphical user interface with several examples.

The following topics will be covered in this chapter:

- Working with classical networks
- Using residual networks for image recognition
- The power of 1 x 1 convolutions and the inception network
- Applying transfer learning
- Building an animal image classification application

Working with classical networks

In this section, we'll go through some of the most used and impactful convolutional neural networks in use today. We'll start with the classical LeNet-5, before moving move on to the more complex AlexNet, and finally we'll see VGG-16, which will be used many times during the course of this book.

LeNet-5

LeNet-5 is a classical neural network architecture that was successfully used on a handwritten digit recognition problem back in 1998. In principle, LeNet-5 was the first architecture that introduced the idea of applying several convolution layers before connecting to a fully-connected hidden layer. Before that, people would construct the features manually and then connect to a simple neural network with many hidden layers and neurons.

Here's the LeNet 5 architecture:

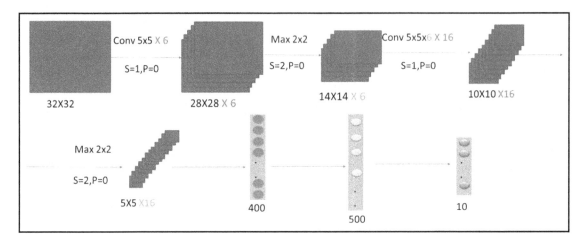

According to the paper, http://users.cecs.anu.edu.au/~Tom.Gedeon/conf/ABCs2018/paper/ABCs2018_paper_57.pdf, this model was able to achieve 99.05% accuracy, which is quite impressive considering the processing power available at the time wasn't good, and it has approximately 60,000 parameters. The architecture will look very similar to what we have worked with previously in this book. We'll use it to build a Java application for a handwritten digit recognition problem.

AlexNet

AlexNet is a modern architecture, from 2012, which works on RGB images and has way more convolution and fully-connected neurons. It's similar to LeNet-5, but AlexNet is bigger and deeper because the processing power in 2012 was quite good and during that time even GPU was created and used in the architecture, which gave really good results.

The following diagram depicts an AlexNet:

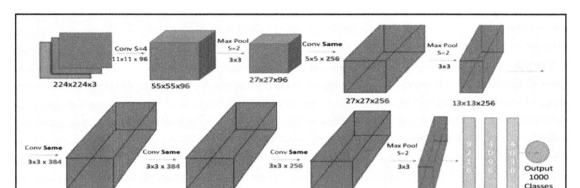

So before we take a layer-by-layer tour of the architecture, there is one dimension that needs modification. When we look at the dimensions for the first convolution at the input layer, we see 11 x 11 x 96. The third dimension here should be exactly the same as the input. This implies that the output obtained from the first convolution layer having stride 4 should be 11 x 11 x 3 x 96. The reason the value is the same, is because the filters to apply the convolution separately for each of the channels of the input should be equal to the input.

We start with of **224 x 224 x 3** RGB image, and then apply a convolution having a stride value of 4 and a filter of **11 x 11 x 3** (where we don't show "x 96" for the reason mentioned previously). After we perform convolution, we have **55 x 55 x 96**; the number of third-dimensional channels dramatically increases to 96, which is equal to the number of filters.

Post this, we apply a max pooling stride of 2 and a filter of 3 x 3, which simply shrinks the first two dimensions but leaves the third one untouched, giving us an output of 27 x 27 x 96. After applying a convolution with the same dimensions of 5 x 5, we, we obtain the output of 27 x 27 x 256.

The same **convolution** does not change the value of the dimension; it uses the convolutional formula and gives us an output the same as the input.

The total number of channels has now been increased to 256. To shrink the first two dimensions but leave the third dimension at 256, we use a max pooling layer having a stride of 2 and then use the convolution same with dimensions 3 x 3 x 384, and increase the third dimension further to 13 x 13 x 384.

Applying a convolution same, we again obtain **3 x 3 x 384,** leaving the number of channels as it was. We then apply a convolution same with dimensions of **3 x 3 x 256**, leading to a decrease in the number of channels since we obtain 13 x 13 x 256. After that, we use max pooling with, stride of 2 and dimensions of 3 x 3 to decrease these first two dimensions even more, and leave the third, dimension 256, untouched.

Let's understand why we choose each of these values and dimensions:

We begin with the first two dimensions, **224 x 224**, and the final output has dimensions of 6 x 6, whereas the number of channels began at 3 and concluded at 256.

This is a typical technique in convolution architectures. We tend to decrease the first two dimensions, but increase the number of channels significantly, because we want to capture more features.

Then, we'll have 3 hidden layers of neurons; the first layer has 9,216 neurons, while the following two layers have 4,096. In the end, we'll try to predict 1,000 classes rather than just 10. This architecture gives us really great results for the first time and, therefore, a lot of people were convinced that deep learning works well for image problems. It has approximately 60,000,000 parameters, basically 100 times more than LeNet-5.

VGG-16

The following architecture of VGG-16 was developed in the year 2015 by K. Simonyan and A. Zisserman from the University of Oxford. It not only has more parameters, but it's also more uniform and simpler to reason:

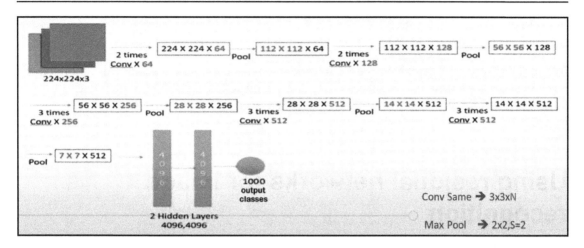

Instead of having different sizes of filters, as AlexNet does, it has the same type of filters, so it has a **convolution same**, 3 x 3, and it has a max pooling of 2 x 2, with a stride of two. When we talk about convolution, we'll always have a 3 x 3, **convolution same**, and when we say pool, we'll always have a max pooling of 2 x 2 with a stride of 2, which usually divides the first 2 dimensions by 2, while the same convolutional leaves the first 2-dimensions untouched but changes the number of channels.

Here is how the VGG-16 works:

1. It has an input of dimension **224 x 224 x 3**, a convolution layer of 64 is applied twice, which is a convolution same having dimensions of **3 x 3 x 64**. The output will be such that the first two dimensions are the same, but the number of channels will be 64.
2. We apply a max pooling that divides this by 2, which gives us 112 x 112 x 64.
3. We apply a convolution of 128, twice, which leaves the first 2 dimensions untouched and changes the third dimension to 112 x 112 x 128.
4. We then apply a pool having a stride of two, giving us the output dimension 56 x 56 x 128.
5. This pool and convolution combination is applied until the first 2 dimensions turn 14, post which, we apply 3 convolutions of 512, and leave everything untouched.
6. The final step entails using a pool to decrease the first 2 dimensions and leave the number of channels untouched.

Observe how similar this strategy is to AlexNet. We started with 224 x 224, and we end up with 7 x 7, while the number of channels increased dramatically from 3 to 512.

For a VGG-16, we connect to 2 heightened, fully-connected layers, each having 4,096 neurons. With AlexNet, we have three of them, with one containing 9,000.

In a manner similar to AlexNet, we try to predict 1,000 output classes, and this architecture has 138,000,000 parameters, approximately 3 times more than AlexNet, which had 60,000,000 parameters. VGG-16 not only has better accuracy, but is also quite simple to extend.

Using residual networks for image recognition

In this section, we're going to see what happens when we train deep networks, which has many layers, probably over 30 or maybe even over 100. Then, we'll present residual networks as a solution for scaling too many layers, along with an architecture example with state-of-the-art accuracy.

Deep network performance

In theory, it's clear that the more layers we add to the neuron network, the better it is. This is the case with the green line, as shown in the following graph. As soon as we add more layers, we'll see the error rate go down, ideally to zero. Unfortunately, in practice, we see this happening only partially. It's true that the error rate goes down once we add more layers, but only until a certain point. After this point, adding more layers will basically increase the error rate:

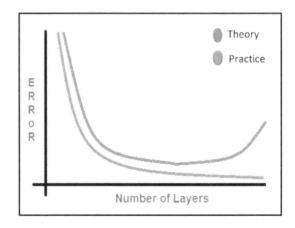

By adding many layers, we add a lot of weights and parameters, making it difficult for the neural network to figure all these weights out. This is one of the reasons why the error rate may go up. Also, there is one more problem, which we saw in the first section: the vanishing gradient. We saw a way to mitigate the problem but not how to solve it; adding more layers will make this problem more obvious and harder to fix. One of the ways to solve this problem is by using residual neural networks:

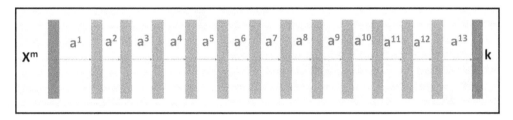

Let's suppose that we have a normal neural network, with m pixels as the input and k as the output. The k could be 1,000, as for `ImageNet`, and then we add many hidden layers. These hidden layers could be either convolution or fully-connected layers. For each of the layers, we have activations. Let's recall the activation where the result such as the ReLU was obtained by applying one of the chosen activation function to the sum of multiplied weights with the previous activation functions.

For example, we calculated a2 in a similar manner as a1 that is, the previous activation function was multiplied by the weights of that respective layer and then, on the result, we apply activation functions like ReLU:

$$a^2 = F(a^1 * w^2)$$

For a3, we have the previous activation multiplied by the third weight at that layer:

$$a^3 = F(a^2 * w^3)$$

And for the tenth layer, we have the previous activation multiplied by the weights at the tenth layer.

$$a^{10} = F(a^9 * w^{10})$$

It is depicted as follows:

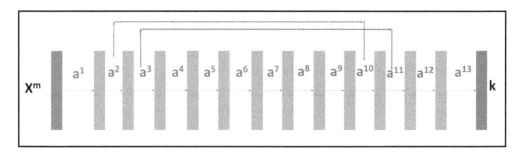

Here, a and w—the weights and the activation, respectively—are matrices. The multiplication has a sum in the middle (the definition we said previously), so the sum of weight multiplication and the previous activation functions holds true.

The problem with the vanishing gradient, for example, was that the gradients were so small that it caused this product to be really small, and that made it very hard for the neural network to find good weights. This is why we have this increase in the error rate. Residual networks solved this error by forwarding earlier activations to deeper layers. Suppose it forwards a^2 to the 10th layer. And by *forward*, we mean that we simply add a^2 to this product. Then, notice how the vanishing gradient was solved in this case. Because even if this product is small, a^2 is big enough, because it comes from the earlier layers. And, at the same time, even if this product was small, it had an impact on the learning process. Like when there is a positive impact, that impact is preserved, which means that it is not lost, since we add that (even if it is small) to the a^2.

By preserving these small contributions in the deeper layers, residual networks keep improving even if we keep adding layers. In contrast to the normal neural network, where the performance degrades when we add more layers, in residual networks, they keep improving, and that's basically because of these early layers' contributions to the deeper layers. For example, for this a^{11}, it may appear something like the following:

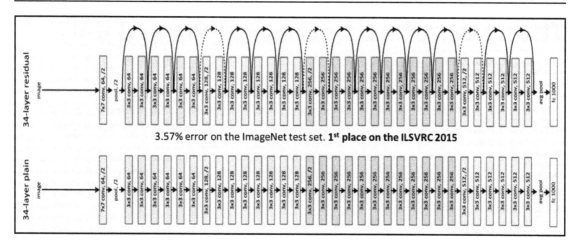

3.57% error on the ImageNet test set. **1st place on the ILSVRC 2015**

a^3 is coming to help a^{11} to have sufficiently large values, for example, if we are facing the vanishing gradients, and if a^{10} multiplied by v^{11} has any good contributions, we preserve those.

ResNet-50

One of the successful architectures that uses the residual networks is ResNet-50, and it took first place in 2015 on the `ImageNet` dataset, with 1,000 classes. The error rate was quite low, that is, 3.57%. It was a simple architecture, because it uses the **convolution same**, like VGG-16, and max pooling. It applies these previous activations to deeper layers and then repeats this for every layer. It has only one different trick that we didn't mention previously: once you use the pooling layer, in contrast to the convolution same, the pooling layer doesn't preserve the first two dimensions but shrinks them, by dividing by two. That causes an obstacle, because you can't simply forward this activation to the further activation layers; they have different dimensions now. One way to balance these dimensions is to use padding with zero, or maybe you can multiply these activations by another vector, just to have the same dimensions as the deeper-layer activations. In this ResNet-50, we have three of these tricks, and the trick, once again, is that it's used only when you use the pooling. Then, you shrink the first two dimensions and you need to balance the weights that you are going to forward to deeper layers, since they have two different dimensions.

The power of 1 x 1 convolutions and the inception network

In this section, we'll see how a 1 x 1 convolution will enable us to build a really interesting network architecture, that is, the inception network. Also, we'll go through the details of why a 1 x 1 convolution is so efficient, and see how GoogLeNet is built on top of this.

First, let's go through a 1 x 1 convolution. It looks really simple, but is very useful. For example, let's assume that we have a **4 x 4 x 1** input matrix and we want to convolve that with a 1 x 1 stride one filter, and, for the sake of argument, let's suppose that the cell value is 4, so it's just a constant:

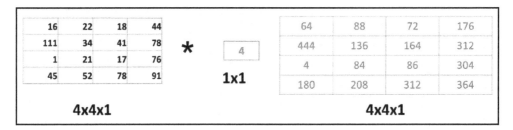

Then, the convolution will be effected as follows:

1. We start with the top-left position and just multiply the cell value by 4, that is 16 * 4, and the result is 64, as highlighted in the following screenshot:

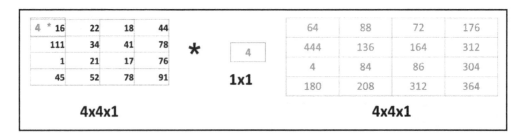

Then as we move right, to the second cell, we multiply it by 4, and we get 88, as shown in the following screenshot:

16	4 * 22	18	44
111	34	41	78
1	21	17	76
45	52	78	91

4x4x1

*

4

1x1

64	88	72	176
444	136	164	312
4	84	86	304
180	208	312	364

4x4x1

Then again, as we move to the right and multiple the third cell value by 4, we have 72:

16	22	4 * 18	44
111	34	41	78
1	21	17	76
45	52	78	91

4x4x1

*

4

1x1

64	88	72	176
444	136	164	312
4	84	86	304
180	208	312	364

4x4x1

Similarly, we get 176 in the fourth cell, as shown in the following screenshot:

16	22	18	4 * 44
111	34	41	78
1	21	17	76
45	52	78	91

4x4x1

*

4

1x1

64	88	72	176
444	136	164	312
4	84	86	304
180	208	312	364

4x4x1

Since we can't go any further to the right, we go 1 step down, and we have 4 multiplied by 111, which makes 444, as is highlighted in the following screenshot:

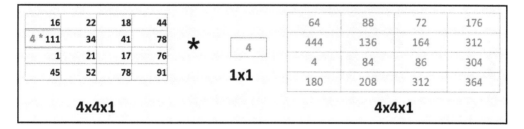

16	22	18	44
4 * 111	34	41	78
1	21	17	76
45	52	78	91

4x4x1

*

4

1x1

64	88	72	176
444	136	164	312
4	84	86	304
180	208	312	364

4x4x1

Then we go right, and then again down, until we end up in the bottom-right cell, which is the last one and makes 364.

The output matrix was just multiplying the input by 4. Even if we let the neural network figure out this value, it will still be multiplied by the constant, and it doesn't look very useful. Let's see another example; instead of having 1 channel, let's suppose that we have 64 channels, as shown in the following diagram. This means that we also need to have a **1 x 1 x 64** filter. The number of channels must match. And this filter will move on this input, for example, at this position. What it will do is multiply all the selected cells and then it will total them up, and all this will produce just one value:

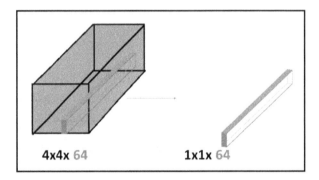

Before producing the sum, we may apply a ReLU function. We saw that we just total this up, but usually, with a 1 x 1 convolution, you apply it to a ReLU function and then the output is sent to the output matrix. Then, we move to another position and do the same thing. We multiply, we sum, and we put this to a ReLU function, and then put it as the output. We will apply many of these 1 x 1 x 64 values, and together we should obtain 4 x 4 x 64, which is depicted in the following diagram:

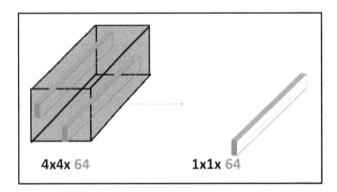

For example, if we suppose the third dimension is 128, we will obtain an output of 4 x 4 x 128.

Now it's clear that a 1 x 1 convolution is really useful. It did a certain amount of multiplication summing, and even used ReLU to figure out more complex functions; at the same time, it increased the number of channels in order to capture more features. But one question still remains: we can do all this with 5 x 5 or 3 x 3 filters too, so what's so special about this 1 x 1 convolution? In order to see that, let's suppose that we have an input matrix with 4 x 4 x 128, and we want an output of 4 x 4 x 32:

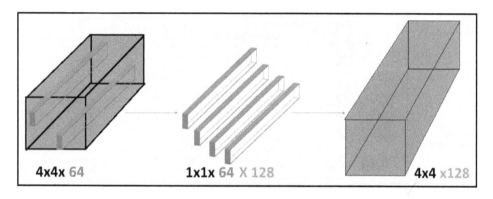

One way to achieve that is by using a convolution same, 5 x 5 x 32. So, **4 x 4 x 128** is multiplied by the filter dimensions of 5 x 5 x 32, which gives us 1.64 million multiplication operations.

Now, let's try to do it a bit differently. Before applying this filter, let's suppose that we apply the convolution of 1 x 1 x 16, and that gives us a 4 x 4 x 16 output, as shown in the following diagram. Let's count the number of multiplications here:

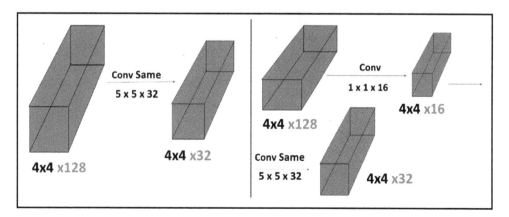

Again, it will be these numbers multiplied together, and this gives us 33,000 multiplications. Now we apply the convolution same of **5 x 5 x 32.** As shown in the preceding diagram it gives us exactly what we want, which is a **4 x 4 x 32** output. Let's count the number of multiplications, which makes 240,000 multiplications, as shown in the following screenshot:

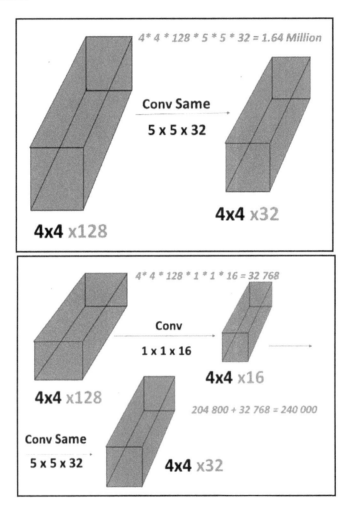

It's much less than the 1,640,000 shown in the preceding diagram, and it was approximately seven times smaller than the number of multiplications when we use a convolution same directly. In reality, the difference would be even more dramatic, because these two dimensions aren't that low. We saw that for RGB and the VGG-16, these were 224 x 224. Sometimes, the difference is 10 times and this could be like 10 millionths of 15 minutes and it's just 1,000,000. Now notice how this 1 x 1 x 16 convolution acted as a kind of bottleneck; somehow, it relaxed the dimensions a bit, when we apply the more expensive filter, it didn't blow up to millions of operations, it lowered down a bit, and then we applied an extensive filter. It's just a bottleneck to lower the computational cost.

Let's understand the inner workings of the inception network depicted in the following diagram:

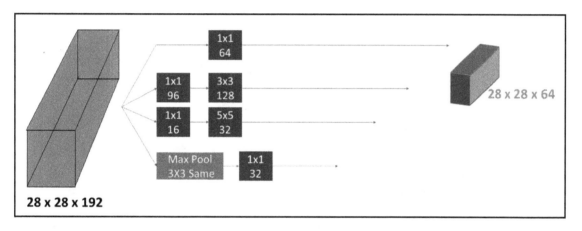

The working is as follows:

1. The first step is to apply a bottleneck, as we've learned to lower the computational cost. To supply the bottleneck, we apply a max pooling of 3 x 3.
2. Apply more expensive filters, such as 3 x 3 and 5 x 5, but in this case, we're comfortable with a 1 x 1 convolution. Each of them separately will produce an output based on the filter used. The first two dimensions stay the same. After we concatenate all of these values, we should have an output of 28 x 28 x 256.

 Notice how the first two dimensions are always kept the same during these operations because it's easier to stack them together. In order to keep these two dimensions the same, we can do all sorts of manipulations, such as budding and reducing dimensions.

GoogLeNet uses several of these blocks together, and this output is just to measure the occurrence in the middle of the network, near the end, and maybe at the beginning. It's to see whether the progress from one layer to the deeper layers has been meaningful. Basically, you can just keep this block out and GoogLeNet just applies these blocks together. And merely a 1 x 1 convolution in 2015, enabled GoogLeNet to have a much deeper architecture and achieve outstanding results.

Applying transfer learning

In this section, we'll discuss transfer learning and how we can use it to train our model easily and more efficiently. Transfer learning is the abstraction of knowledge from the original owner, in such a way that anyone can obtain it freely. In a way, it's similar to how humans transfer knowledge between generations, or to each other.

Originally, for humans, the only way to transfer experience was by talking. As you can imagine, this was crucial for our survival. Of course, we eventually found better ways of storing knowledge, that is, through writing. In this way, we preserved the knowledge in its original form for a longer period, making it more extendable. Even nowadays, the dissemination of information is a fundamental aspect of society. Almost every mathematical theory is built on top of existing ones, which were written years ago.

Now we are in the era of digitalization. Information is disseminated much faster, reaching a significant number of people. We're talking about the internet, social media, online learning, and access to information everywhere, at any time. Regardless of its evolution, the basic concept behind knowledge transferal is the same. There's abstraction of information from the owner, and then we preserve it in a form where anyone can obtain it. First, we stored it in memory, that is, in people's brains; and then in books, that is, on paper by writing it down; and finally in the electronic format, that is, in the format where other humans can freely access and read it:

Neural networks

As we saw in the first section of the chapter, all neural networks are learning the weights in each of the layers. Maybe we have millions of weights, but what a neural network is trying to figure out are good values. For example, first we do the forward pass, during which we generate the hypothesis. Then we compare the hypothesis with the real values of the data we have, and then come back with feedback that will change the weights in a way that the next forward pass will produce a better hypothesis. This feedback pass, or the backpropagation pass, updates all the weights:

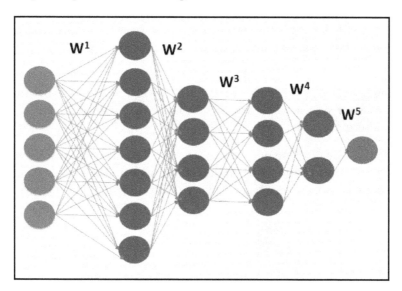

We repeat this process of the forward pass and the backpropagation pass until we're satisfied with the accuracy:

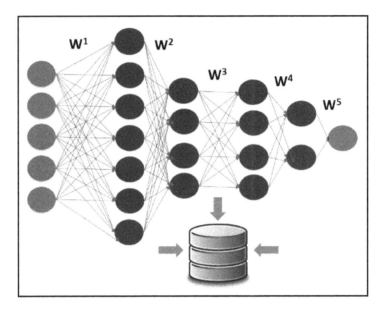

Now, if we store all these decimal values of the weights in the disk, in some way, we are storing all the knowledge of this neural network to resolve the problem in hand. This means that if any other neural network with the same configuration or number of neurons and hidden layers loads these decimal values or these weights, it will be able to predict the results with the exact same accuracy. The knowledge is completely abstracted from the original neural network, which is the first strength. Every other neural network can then load the knowledge or the parameters, and can improve from there by continuing to train even further.

Transfer learning knowledge is independent from the technical details because, in the end, we don't store any source code or binary code as is the case with software, just pure decimal values. Therefore, any program written in a

ny technology that can read those decimal values will have all the knowledge of solving the problem, and indeed some of the words we'll use in this book come from the C++ neural network, Python, or TensorFlow, which are very different from Java frameworks.

The ways we can use the power of transfer learning depend mostly on two factors: the amount and quality of the data we have at hand, and the processing power we can afford. For computer vision, I would say, as a default choice, that it's better to first look around; maybe someone else already trained a network for the problem we want to solve, or maybe a similar problem. Someone may have trained the neural network for weeks or even months, and has already gone through the painful process of parameter tuning, and you can reuse all that work and maybe take it from there to improve it further.

Let's suppose we have a neural network with an input, hidden layers, and the softmax layer that tries to predict 1,000 classes, as shown in the following diagram. Let's take the first example, when we don't have a lot of data and we can't afford a lot of processing power. In this case, we'll load the weights from a pre-trained neural network, and we'll freeze up all the weights in all the hidden layers. What we mean by freeze is that we aren't going to train these weights:

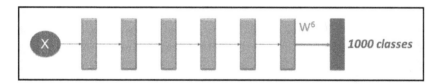

We're going to use the weight values for the forward pass, and when we get the feedback, we'll stop. We aren't going to update all the millions of weights used here. Therefore, it's clear that we aren't using up any processing power.

We can even go one step further by modifying this softmax layer. Instead of outputting 1,000 classes we modify the output. For example, consider two classes, if we're trying to solve a problem such as determining whether the image is of a dog or a cat. Now, we'll train only these weights. Perhaps these weights may number 1,000 classes, but they'll be much lower than millions of weights, as in VGG-16 for example.

Then we have the second case, where we have a bit more data than before but still not enough, but we can afford more processing power:

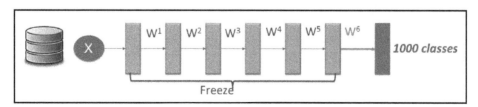

Usually, we can load pre-trained weights from a neural network somewhere, but in this case, we freeze fewer layers, as shown in the preceding diagram, and we'll train the rest of the weights. For the forward pass, we'll reuse all the layers at once and go straight to the end, and when we come back with some feedback, with the backpropagation step, we'll update all these weights. Instead of stopping here, we'll go to the fourth layer and stop there. Sometimes, this produces better results because we're adapting these weights more accurately to our problem, since we're training more weights. Or we can say that we're improving the existing weights:

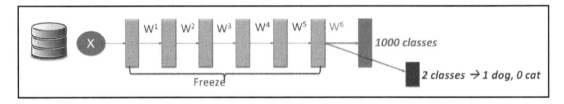

Then we have a case where we have a lot of data and we're sure about its quality. It'll bring something better to our problem, and, at the same time, we can afford a lot of processing power. In this case, we load the weights from a neural network, but we don't freeze any of the layers. So we just get these weights and then train our data again and again. Of course, we need to modify the softmax most of the time, because we're trying to predict different classes. Even when you have a lot of resources to train a neural network from scratch, using the weights won't hurt if the problems are sufficiently similar. You can still reuse some of the features the neural network is capturing there. In the next section, we'll see how to build a Java application that's able to recognize cats and dogs, and we'll use the first case, where we don't have a lot of data and processing power.

Building an animal image classification – using transfer learning and VGG-16 architecture

In this section, we're going to build a cat-and-dog recognizer Java application using the VGG-16 architecture and transfer learning. Let's revisit the VGG-16 architecture (explained previously in the *Working with classical networks* section).

The VGG-16 architecture is quite uniform; we have only one 3 x 3 same convolution, which leaves the first 2 dimensions untouched and increases the number of channels in the third dimension, and also increases the max pooling 2 x 2 stride two, which, in turn, decreases the first 2 dimensions by dividing it by 2, thereby leaving the third dimension untouched. The idea with many convolution architectures is eventually to shrink these two-dimensions and increase the number of channels; if we look at the output of these convolution layers from 224 x 224 x 3, we end up with 7 x 7 x 512. Then, in the next step, we connect all these to 2 fully-connected hidden layers, each of them with 4,096 neurons. Finally, we use a softmax to predict 1,000 classes, which is the same case with `ImageNet`.

With transfer learning, we will first freeze all these layers. These weights won't be trained any more, but we'll use the pre-trained values that they were trained on, for example, the `ImageNet` dataset. After that, we'll do another modification, since we don't need 1,000 classes, but just 2. We'll replace the softmax to predict only cats and dogs. The number of trainable parameters will be reduced only to these ones here, which, as we'll see in the code, is just 2 multiplied by 4,096. Let's jump into the code and see how we can do all this using Java and Deeplearning4j.

First, we start with some familiar parameters, the number of epochs and the learning rate, as shown in the following screenshot:

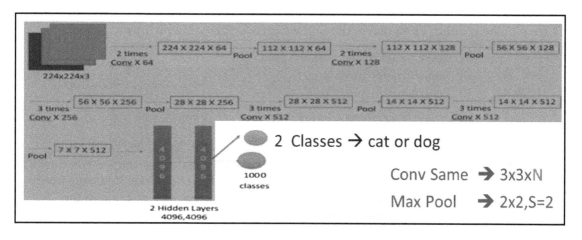

While the freeze layer is quite important, we'll learn more about it as we proceed. The first step is to load the VGG-16 architecture and the pre-trained weights. That's quite easy; the constructor prepares everything, but will have no weights there; in order to load the pre-trained weights that you can find at the `CatVsDogREcognition.java` file, this method needs to be called as follows:

```
public CatVsDogRecognition() throws IOException {
  this.computationGraph = loadModel();
  computationGraph.init();
  log.info(computationGraph.summary());
  }
public AnimalType detectAnimalType(File file, Double threshold) throws
IOException {
  INDArray image = imageFileToMatrix(file);
  INDArray output = computationGraph.outputSingle(false, image);
  if (output.getDouble(0) > threshold) {
  return AnimalType.CAT;
  } else if (output.getDouble(1) > threshold) {
  return AnimalType.DOG;
  } else {
  return AnimalType.NOT_KNOWN;
  }
  }
```

Then, plot the weights, as shown in the following code snippet, which were gained by training with `ImageNet`:

```
public class CatVsDogRecognition {
  public static final String TRAINED_PATH_MODEL = DataStorage.DATA_PATH +
"/model.zip";
  private ComputationGraph computationGraph;
```

`ImageNet` has a huge dataset, with millions of images. Just through these two lines, as mentioned in the preceding code block, we get the benefit of using pre-trained weights in a huge dataset; a big team of developers actually trained it for a really long time and went through the painful process of choosing the best parameters that you can find in the `TransferLearningVGG16.java` file, as follows:

```
public class TransferLearningVGG16 {
  private static final int SAVING_INTERVAL = 100;
/**
  * Number of total traverses through data.
  * with 5 epochs we will have 5/@MINI_BATCH_SIZE iterations or weights
updates
  */
  private static final int EPOCH = 5;
```

```
/**
 * The layer where we need to stop back propagating
 */
private static final String FREEZE_UNTIL_LAYER = "fc2";
/**
 * The alpha learning rate defining the size of step towards the minimum
 */
private static final double LEARNING_RATE = 5e-5;
private NeuralNetworkTrainingData neuralNetworkTrainingData;
```

Then, we'll print the structure of the VGG-16 architecture, which will be in the form of a table. Then, we'll download the data which will be used to train this modifier or this transfer learning VGG-16 architecture:

```
private ComputationGraph loadVGG16PreTrainedWeights() throws IOException {
  ZooModel zooModel = new VGG16();
  log.info("Start Downloading VGG16 model...");
  return (ComputationGraph)
zooModel.initPretrained(PretrainedType.IMAGENET);
  }
private void unzip(File fileZip) {
Unzip unZip = new Unzip();
  unZip.setSrc(fileZip);
  unZip.setDest(new File(DATA_PATH));
  unZip.execute();
  }
```

In this method, we aren't going into the details. But it's quite easy; we just download some data and unzip it to a folder. After we download the data, which is in a row format, we need a way to structure it into the training dataset, the development dataset, and the test dataset.

Just to recall, the training dataset is the set used to train or optimize our weights. The developer set is used to see how to generalize the unseen data and some optimizations. The test dataset, which isn't often used for small projects, is just to get an unbiased evaluation for the data that the neural network has never seen nor optimized. How to recall this dataset is demonstrated in the following code block:

```
public void train() throws IOException {
  ComputationGraph preTrainedNet = loadVGG16PreTrainedWeights();
  log.info("VGG 16 Architecture");
  log.info(preTrainedNet.summary());
  log.info("Start Downloading NeuralNetworkTrainingData...");
  downloadAndUnzipDataForTheFirstTime();
  log.info("NeuralNetworkTrainingData Downloaded and unzipped");
  neuralNetworkTrainingData = new DataStorage() {
  }.loadData();
```

In this case, we'll sample the training data through 85%, which will be used for training, and the rest will be used for the development of datasets at 50%. As we continue, all the `test` datasets will be used for tests or 100% of them, as shown in the following code:

```
private void downloadAndUnzipDataForTheFirstTime() throws IOException {
File data = new File(DATA_PATH + "/data.zip");
if (!data.exists() || FileUtils.checksum(data, new Adler32()).getValue()
!= 1195241806) {
data.delete();
FileUtils.copyURLToFile(new URL(ONLINE_DATA_URL), data);
log.info("File downloaded");
}
if (!new File(TRAIN_DIRECTORY_PATH).exists()) {
log.info("Unzipping NeuralNetworkTrainingData...");
unzip(data);
}
}
```

Then, we have the fine-tuned configuration (executed in the following code block and that can be found in the `DataStorage.java` file in the repo), which is just a collection of the parameters used for training more effectively than a network:

```
FineTuneConfiguration fineTuneConf = new FineTuneConfiguration.Builder()
.learningRate(LEARNING_RATE)
.optimizationAlgo(OptimizationAlgorithm.STOCHASTIC_GRADIENT_DESCENT)
.updater(Updater.NESTEROVS)
.seed(1234)
.build();
```

As we have seen before, this training is for the momentum updater and the learning rate. Also, the stochastic gradient descent is used with the mini-batch for training the model:

```
default NeuralNetworkTrainingData loadData() throws IOException {
InputSplit[] trainAndDevData = TRAIN_DATA.sample(PATH_FILTER, TRAIN_SIZE,
100 - TRAIN_SIZE);
return new
NeuralNetworkTrainingData(getDataSetIterator(trainAndDevData[0]),
getDataSetIterator(trainAndDevData[1]),
getDataSetIterator(TEST_DATA.sample(PATH_FILTER, 1, 0)[0]));
}
```

Then we have the modified version of the VGG-16 architecture, which is where we apply the transfer learning. We'll use a transfer learning graph builder. The first method is just to give a reference to the fine-tuned configuration, and the second method is quite important. Here, we instruct Deeplearning4j to freeze the layers, and this fc2 is just a fully-connected layer two. If we print the VGG-16 architecture before the modification, the output will be in the form of a table, and, in the end, we have fc2.

This method freezes everything up to this layer. All these layers will be frozen, as we saw in this section, including the fc2 itself. Hence, this will no longer be trained.

And then this second method stipulates removal of the predictions, since we have 1,000 classes, and to replace this original prediction with another prediction, which provides a softmax layer with two classes as an output: dog and cat. We'll use a softmax layer with the Xavier initialization. If we print the modified architecture, which is shown in the following code block and can be found under the `TransferLearningVGG16.java` file in the repo, we can see that this 1,000 was reduced to 2, while the number of parameters was reduced as well:

```
ComputationGraph vgg16Transfer = new
TransferLearning.GraphBuilder(preTrainedNet)
  .fineTuneConfiguration(fineTuneConf)
  .setFeatureExtractor(FREEZE_UNTIL_LAYER)
  .removeVertexKeepConnections("predictions")
  .addLayer("predictions",
  new OutputLayer.Builder(LossFunctions.LossFunction.NEGATIVELOGLIKELIHOOD)
  .nIn(4096)
  .nOut(NUM_POSSIBLE_LABELS)
  .weightInit(WeightInit.XAVIER)
  .activation(Activation.SOFTMAX)
  .build(),
  FREEZE_UNTIL_LAYER)
  .build();
vgg16Transfer.setListeners(new ScoreIterationListener(5));
```

Notice how the trainable parameters were 138,000,000 in the original architecture, and are now reduced to 8,194. This number is calculated in accordance with the number of classes multiplied by the fully-connected layer, fc2. This gives us 8,192 plus 2 biases:

VertexName (VertexType)	nIn,nOut	TotalParams	ParamsShape	Vertex Inputs
input_1 (InputVertex)	-,-	-	-	-
block1_conv1 (ConvolutionLayer)	3,64	1792	b:(1,64), W:(64,3,3,3)	[input_1]
block1_conv2 (ConvolutionLayer)	64,64	36928	b:(1,64), W:(64,64,3,3)	[block1_conv1]
block1_pool (SubsamplingLayer)	-,-	0	-	[block1_conv2]
block2_conv1 (ConvolutionLayer)	64,128	73856	b:(1,128), W:(128,64,3,3)	[block1_pool]
block2_conv2 (ConvolutionLayer)	128,128	147584	b:(1,128), W:(128,128,3,3)	[block2_conv1]
block2_pool (SubsamplingLayer)	-,-	0	-	[block2_conv2]
block3_conv1 (ConvolutionLayer)	128,256	295168	b:(1,256), W:(256,128,3,3)	[block2_pool]
block3_conv2 (ConvolutionLayer)	256,256	590080	b:(1,256), W:(256,256,3,3)	[block3_conv1]
block3_conv3 (ConvolutionLayer)	256,256	590080	b:(1,256), W:(256,256,3,3)	[block3_conv2]
block3_pool (SubsamplingLayer)	-,-	0	-	[block3_conv3]
block4_conv1 (ConvolutionLayer)	256,512	1180160	b:(1,512), W:(512,256,3,3)	[block3_pool]

We reduce the number of parameters dramatically, and this will speed up our training. At the same time, we have these weights, which we trained in a huge dataset. We have the benefits of capturing various types of features already, demonstrated as follows:

```
block4_conv2 (ConvolutionLayer)    512,512      2359808    b:{1,512},  W:{512,512,3,3}    [block4_conv1]
block4_conv3 (ConvolutionLayer)    512,512      2359808    b:{1,512},  W:{512,512,3,3}    [block4_conv2]
block4_pool (SubsamplingLayer)     -,-          0          -                              [block4_conv3]
block5_conv1 (ConvolutionLayer)    512,512      2359808    b:{1,512},  W:{512,512,3,3}    [block4_pool]
block5_conv2 (ConvolutionLayer)    512,512      2359808    b:{1,512},  W:{512,512,3,3}    [block5_conv1]
block5_conv3 (ConvolutionLayer)    512,512      2359808    b:{1,512},  W:{512,512,3,3}    [block5_conv2]
block5_pool (SubsamplingLayer)     -,-          0          -                              [block5_conv3]
flatten (PreprocessorVertex)       -,-          -          -                              [block5_pool]
fc1 (DenseLayer)                   25088,4096   102764544  b:{1,4096}, W:{25088,4096}     [flatten]
fc2 (DenseLayer)                   4096,4096    16781312   b:{1,4096}, W:{4096,4096}      [fc1]
predictions (DenseLayer)           4096,1000    4097000    b:{1,1000}, W:{4096,1000}      [fc2]
```

After modifying the architecture, we're ready to train the model. This training code here is quite similar to what we saw in the preceding code block. We'll use the mini-batch sizes to train and then we'll save our progress and evaluate the development dataset for the configure interval. Here, we'll save the model every 100 iterations, and see how it's doing.

We'll evaluate every single epoch in the `test` dataset, and get the stats.

Then, the best model will be used by this implementation, which is quite straightforward:

```
=========================================================================================================
VertexName (VertexType)                     nIn,nOut    TotalParams    ParamsShape                Vertex Inputs
=========================================================================================================
input_1 (InputVertex)                       -,-         -              -                          -
block1_conv1 (Frozen ConvolutionLayer)      3,64        1792           b:{1,64},  W:{64,3,3,3}     [input_1]
block1_conv2 (Frozen ConvolutionLayer)      64,64       36928          b:{1,64},  W:{64,64,3,3}    [block1_conv1]
block1_pool (Frozen SubsamplingLayer)       -,-         0              -                          [block1_conv2]
block2_conv1 (Frozen ConvolutionLayer)      64,128      73856          b:{1,128}, W:{128,64,3,3}   [block1_pool]
block2_conv2 (Frozen ConvolutionLayer)      128,128     147584         b:{1,128}, W:{128,128,3,3}  [block2_conv1]
block2_pool (Frozen SubsamplingLayer)       -,-         0              -                          [block2_conv2]
block3_conv1 (Frozen ConvolutionLayer)      128,256     295168         b:{1,256}, W:{256,128,3,3}  [block2_pool]
block3_conv2 (Frozen ConvolutionLayer)      256,256     590080         b:{1,256}, W:{256,256,3,3}  [block3_conv1]
block3_conv3 (Frozen ConvolutionLayer)      256,256     590080         b:{1,256}, W:{256,256,3,3}  [block3_conv2]
block3_pool (Frozen SubsamplingLayer)       -,-         0              -                          [block3_conv3]
```

When it gets the image file, it transforms it into an array, and it will ask the best model for the prediction. It then stipulates what type of image you'd return if one of the predictions exceeds the threshold:

```
Total Parameters:     138357544
Trainable Parameters: 138357544
Frozen Parameters:    0
```

The default value of the threshold is 50%, but when we see it from a graphical user interface, this is configurable. When any type of prediction doesn't exceed the threshold, we'll feel like we don't know what this is.

Summary

In this chapter, we studied the architectures of LeNet-5, AlexNet, VGG-16, and ResNet-50. Then, we discussed transfer learning and how we can use it to train our model easily and efficiently. We also learned how to build a cat-and-dog recognizer Java application using the VGG-16 architecture and transfer learning.

In the next chapter, we'll explore real-time object detection, which performs recognition and marks objects with bounding boxes.

Real-Time Object Detection 4

In this chapter, we're going to solve one of the most challenging problems that arises from computer vision—real-time object detection.

We'll begin by getting familiar with the object localization problem, and learn how to label data and modify the network layer of the neural network to fit this problem. Throughout this chapter, we'll learn how to detect an object with using the sliding window technique and the convolutional window technique. We'll conclude each section by exploring the downsides of the method and how to overcome them. We'll take a closer look at the state-of-the-art algorithm, **You Only Look Once** (**YOLO**), that does a great job of detecting objects. We'll conclude this chapter by building a real-time application for object detection.

In this chapter, we'll cover the following topics:

- Resolving object localization
- Object detection using the sliding window algorithm
- Convolutional sliding window
- Detecting objects using the YOLO algorithm
- Max suppression and anchor boxes
- Building a real-time object detector in Java

Resolving object localization

In this section, we'll look at an interesting solution to solving the object localization and detection problem. In addition, we'll learn how to label data and modify the prediction layer based on the need of the localization problem. We'll extend this to landmark detection, which should enable us to do fascinating things, such as detect a person smiling.

We're familiar with the image classification problem; we need to determine whether the image contains any of the desired classes, such as whether the object is a car or a person. Apart from image recognition, we also want to find the position of the object or localize the object by marking it with a bounding box:

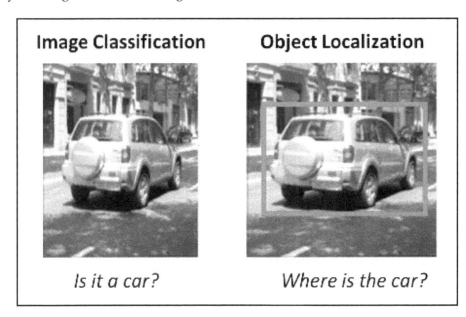

We'll also extend the idea of localization to multiple objects during the course of this chapter.

Labeling and defining data for localization

When labeling data, we need to follow simple binary logic. Whenever an image contains an object that belongs to a particular class that you require, it will label it as 1, and if it doesn't contain an object, it will label it 0. The following image depicts a bounding box around a car:

When it come to object localization, the labeling of the object is more difficult as we have much more information to deal with.

Consider that P_c simply denotes whether this image has any of the classes we want to predict. If it's **1**, this means that we have one of the classes we want to predict, and **0** means we don't have any of them. b_x and b_y mark the center of the bounding box, and b_h and b_w mark the height and width of the bounding box. We also have the class number that's depicted by **C1**, **C2**, **C3**, and so on.

Before we proceed with the process of detection, let's define the coordinates of the image:

The top left corner is **(0,0)** and the bottom right corner is marked as **(1,1)**.

The P_c value signals that we have one of the classes in the image. The coordinates (0.5, 0.5) depict the center of the bounding box and of the image. The height is at **0.5** and the width is measured at **0.8**. Lastly, we have the digit **1**, which depicts that we have a car in the image.

To understand this better, let's consider another example:

$$
\begin{matrix}
P_c & b_x & b_y & b_h & b_w & C1 & C2 & C3 & C4 \\
\end{matrix}
$$
$$
\begin{bmatrix}
1 & 0.5 & 0.5 & 0.4 & 0.8 & 1 & 0 & 0 & 0 \\
0 & ? & ? & ? & ? & ? & ? & ? & ?
\end{bmatrix}
$$

The value of P_c here is **0**, which means that the concerned object is not present in the image. If the value of **Pc** is **0**, we don't need to care about the other values, we simply ignore them.

Object localization prediction layer

Once the data has been labeled, we need to adopt the prediction layer. Let's look at the following flow chart:

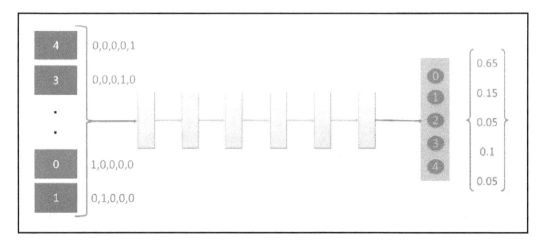

If we consider the image-classifier example used in the previous section, we label the image and depict different images as belonging to different classes.

All of this information is fed to the neural network, which passes through the prediction layer using softmax, and this outputs the probabilities for each class.

The neural network will map the output as 65% chances if it being class 0, 15% chance of the image being class 1, and so on.

During the process of training, we calculate the difference of the real value and the predicted value. This information is used during backpropagation to vary the weights to obtain better predictions.

The next prediction for the same example will be better and more accurate in nature.

With the localization problem, the only difference is the structure of the data. Here's how we define our data:

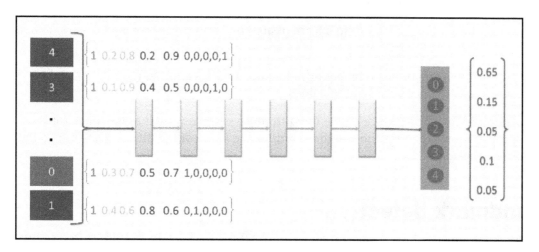

We have P_c, followed by the properties of the bounding box and the class number, which looks identical to the classifier problem.

It's obviously no surprise that the prediction layer has to produce the same structure as the data. Due to this, the P_c value is a bit different because it's a probability:

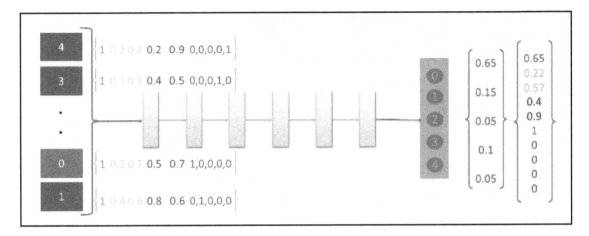

To resolve this, values greater than 0.5 are treated as 1 and those less than 0.5 are treated as 0.

The prediction layer contains the bounding box properties and then the class numbers. We calculate the difference between the values.

Consider the 0 example; we calculate the difference and then use it as feedback for backpropagation to change the weight to reduce the value of the difference between the predicted and real values.

Landmark detection

So far, we've enriched the data with more information, such as the bounding box center, the height, and the width. Providing more detailed information leads to better results, which makes our network smarter.

We can use this concept and label the data with more information. Look at the following screenshot:

Let's use labeling data for face detection in a similar fashion:

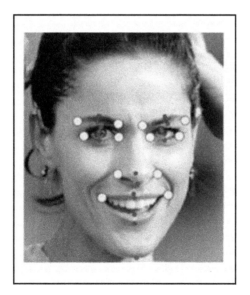

We've marked the crucial points, such as the eyes and mouth. Each of these points is localized by the x-coordinate and the y-coordinate. This will help the network give us information about unseen faces as well.

The labeling of data present in the images is as follows:

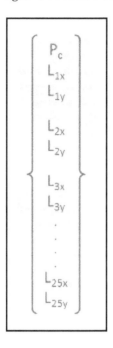

The P_c values can be 1 or 0, denoting whether this image contains a face or not.

By looking at the shapes, we can figure out the emotion expressed by the person. Is the person smiling? Are they serious? Are they angry? Having this information can help us manipulate the image by adding filters, which has a lot of applications use currently.

Object detection with the sliding window solution

In this section, we'll learn to solve the object detection problem of detecting multiple object positions using the sliding window technique. At the end of this section, we'll explore the downsides of using this method.

The very first step is to train a **convolutional neural network (CNN)**as a VGG-16 or maybe a more advanced architecture, such as the inception network, or even the residual network. We'll use cropped images as the training data, instead of the original size of the images. The cropped images will contain only the object in question.

In this example, we'll use the car detection problem and the images will contain cars. When it comes to practical implementation, there are two things that we need to keep in mind:

- It would help if we used different crop sizes for different images.
- Add images other than those of cars as it would help if the neural network knew what an image without a car looks like. We can use images of nature, birds, and so on.

To begin detecting multiple cars or objects with a sliding window algorithm we need to understand the algorithm. The concept of the sliding window is relatively simple.

Begin by choosing different window sizes and bounding boxes that are similar to the sizes of the cropped images that we used to train the model. The second step involves moving or sliding the window across the entire image:

For the sake of this example, let's move the window right, down, and then right again in the next row. Continue this process all the way until the window is at the bottom-right of the image.

We repeat this process for different window sizes and move it in a similar fashion.

The significance of carrying out this step is that the pixel values obtained from this are used as in input to the convolutional network that we trained, which implies that the network is trained with a cropped image.

The network doesn't know that bigger images exist, but it's capable of telling us whether a car is present in the selected pixels given to the network.

For this example, for a random window size, when the window lies on top of a car, it will tell us whether there's a car because the network is also trained with images that don't include cars.

Here are some screenshots of the routine in progress. When you look at the following screenshot, you can see that the pixels bounded in a box in the following image do not contain a car:

The selected pixels contain a car and are thus, marked as red.

The window size can be varied, and each time we give the selected pixels to the CNN, which was trained with cropped images.

Disadvantages of sliding windows

Although the sliding window is a simple algorithm, it has some downsides. The biggest downside is the low performance:

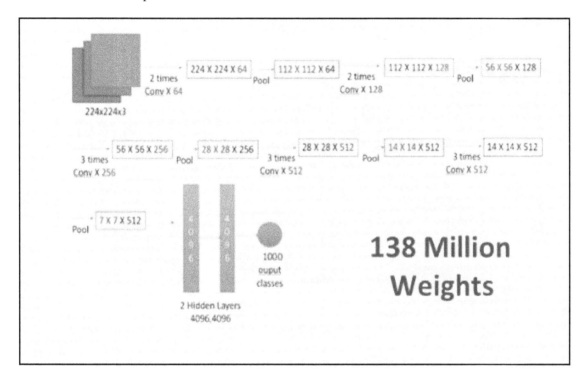

Up until a few years ago, it was OK to use the sliding window, since the features were mostly composed by hand. This meant there were fewer weights to execute.

Now, we have VGG-16, which contains 138,000,000 weights, and these millions of weights need to be executed each time the window moves a step, and we need to do this for different window sizes.

It's clear that this method is almost unusable, especially for real-time object detection.

The second drawback is that the algorithm is quite inefficient. Look at the following screenshot:

The window is moved right and down, and we can observe that the pixels are shared. When using the sliding-window algorithm, each time that we move the window, it doesn't reuse the execution from the previous movement. This means that if pixels here were already executed, when we move the window, we probably end up executing them again. Imagine the number of pixels shared over the entire image and the time and resources used to carry out this execution.

Instead of this, we could reuse the values obtained from the previous execution.

The third drawback is that sometimes the sliding window may not define accurate bounding boxes, as we can see in the following screenshot:

This can be resolved by using a smaller stride or using a completely different window size. Here again, we loop back to the issue where using smaller steps would be inefficient and time consuming.

Convolutional sliding window

In this section, we'll resolve the downsides of using a sliding window by using a convolutional sliding window and gain some intuition behind this technique.

Before we delve into this new method, we need to modify the convolution architecture that we've used so far.

Here is a typical CNN:

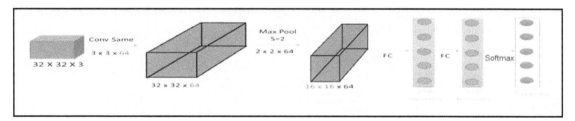

We have the input, an **red, green, and blue** (**RGB**) image with three channels, and here we'll use a small **32 x 32** image. This is followed by a convolution that leaves the first two dimensions unchanged and increases the number of channels to **64**, the max pooling layer divides the first two dimensions by 2, and leaves the number of channels unchanged. In this example, we have two layers. In practical architectures, there are several layers. In the end, we'll have the fully-connected layers with neurons. Here, we have two heightened layers, one with **256** neurons, and the other one with **128** neurons. There is a softmax layer that helps us gain probabilities for the classes we want to predict. We also have five classes.

The modification we'll introduce is to convert these fully-connected layers into convolutional layers. The fully-connected layers have two properties; the first one is that every value of the input is linked to every point in the output, so each of these **16 x 16 x 64** enters as an input to all other points that lie in the first heightened layer. Here, that's all the other **256** neurons. The second property of the fully-connected layer is that before the output is given to the next layer, we apply an activation function, which is a nonlinear function that gives us the ability to learn really complex functions.

This means that all of the values leaving the second heightened layer will be multiplied by the weights, they will be summed up to give only one output, and the values will be given to an activation function.

Let's understand how we can apply the same effect using convolutional layers. The only thing that changes is instead of the fully-connected layer, we use a **16 x 16** convolutional layer:

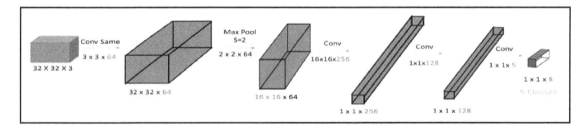

The first two dimensions stay the same and that causes the output to be **1 x 1 x 256**, the **256** matches the number of neurons. Check whether the first property of having every input connected to the output is fulfilled.

If we take the convolution operation into account, the **16 x 16 x 64** values are each multiplied by 16, and now we have the third dimension, which we usually don't show because it's always the same as the input third dimension. Thus, your output will be **16 x 16 x 64**. All the values that pass through the filter will be multiplied by **16 x 16 x 64**. We then sum up all these matrices by gaining only one output, and the output will be this rectangle value. If we apply **256** of these structures of **16 x 16 x 64**, we'll have these **256** rectangles values. Now, notice how every input contributes to the output, so basically the first property of having fully connected layers is achieved.

Next, we apply the **1 x 1 x 128** convolution, which gives us **1 x 1 x 128**, so **128** neurons match this vector. When we used the **1 x 1** convolution, besides multiplying this with all the values and summing up, we also applied an activation function, and we use that as an output of the convolution, which fulfills the second condition of nonlinearity.

We apply the convolution routine, we just use an activation function to the output, and we use the result of the activation function as the final output. And that basically makes our function nonlinear.

Lastly, we apply a **1 x 1 x 5** convolution, and the softmax will enable us to predict **5** classes.

The question that still remains is, if the fully-connected layer and the convolution have the same mathematical effect, why did we feel the need to change this in the first place?

In order to understand that, we use a bigger image; instead of **32 x 32** we use **36 x 36** image:

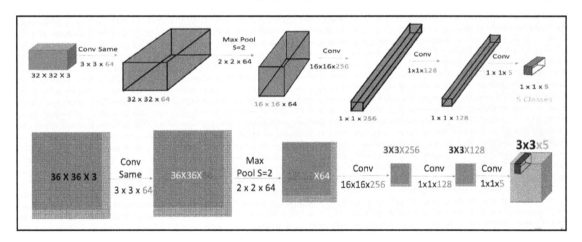

In order for the **32 x 32** image to cover **36 x 36**, we need nine movements. The rectangle depicted in the image rectangle is **32 x 32**, and if we use stride value of **2**, we need nine movements to cover all the pixels in the image.

Now, let's apply the convolutional and max pooling layers. The first convolutional layer increases the number of channels. The max pooling divides and here we need nine movements, or **16 x 16**, to cover *18 x 18*, then by applying the same convolutional layer we have **3 x 3 x 256**. This makes it clear that we need nine movements or **1 x 1** to cover the **3 x 3** matrixes.

Similarly, we apply the same convolutional layer again and obtain **3 x 3 x 128** with nine movements again. Lastly, we apply **1 x 1 x 5**. The output obtained is **3 x 3 x 5**. Notice that the output that we've obtained is similar to having nine movements of **1 x 1 x 5** because the output obtained is **3 x 3 x 9** and we have nine movements to cover the entire structure of **36 x 36** using **32 x 32**.

In a way, we obtain nine predictions with only one network execution for each of these windows. By the end, your window will have moved across the image, like this:

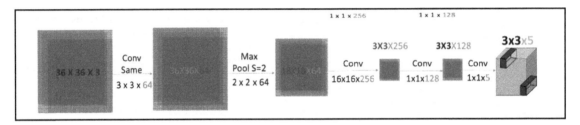

Notice that none of the pixels are being executed again; instead, they are being reused.

When we compare this to the sliding window method, we need to execute them separately. Assume another position, as shown in the following diagram:

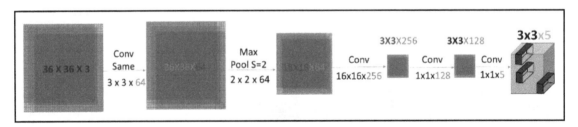

Basically this structure has the prediction for the selected pixels.

To understand this better, let's compare the sliding window with the convolutional sliding window. The picture for the sliding window looked like this:

Several window sizes move to the old image to cover it, and each time the window moves, the selected pieces are given to a neural network and it's asked for a prediction. This means the neural network executes all the weights each time. When we use the convolutional sliding window, with just one execution we add all the predictions, as shown in the following image:

All this is because of the ability to reuse the sharing pixels. This is really a huge improvement, which enables us to do real-time object video detection. Still, even if the performance has improved, we have one last problem: sometimes the sliding algorithm will give an output of an inaccurate bounding box. To resolve this, we'll use YOLO algorithm.

Detecting objects with the YOLO algorithm

In this section, we're going to see how the YOLO algorithm works. YOLO stands for you only look once. The name comes from the fact that you need only one execution of the neural network to get all predictions, which is possible because of the use of convolutional sliding windows.

YOLO solves the problem of the bounding box's accuracy. So as we saw in the previous section, we had this image:

With the help of the convolutional sliding window, we were able to detect all the window's predictions with one execution. So, for each of these windows, we can detect whether the selected pixels represent a car.

Now the problem is that even if we can do that, this window is kind of steady, making it incapable of representing a good bounding box. Observe the image carefully to notice that none of the cars is in a good bounding box.

Looking at this, almost 90% of the window contains non-car information, which isn't good. Here's where YOLO steps in. It lets you specify the bounding boxes freely, where each can cross through several windows:

Let's assume that the dimensions of the bounding boxes are specified relatively to the width and height of an image. Therefore, for the previous image, we can assume the height to be 0.2 or 20% of the height of the image and the width can be 0.1 or 10% of the width of the image. We can define the center of the bounding boxes and then define the boundaries as well. The top-left is (0, 0), the bottom-right is (1,1), and the coordinates of the centers of the bounding boxes will vary per the location of the box.

Once the neural network is fitted with labeled data, the neural network will give you back the same structure. It will predict the structure of the bounding boxes.

There's one problem: we need to connect the bounding boxes to the windows, because what the convolutional sliding window will give you in the end is just the windows. YOLO solves this problem by assigning the bounding boxes' height, width, and center to the window that holds the center of the bounding box.

For example, in such cases, only the windows depicted in the following screenshot will be responsible for detecting an object and having the bounding box specification:

Whichever window contains the center of the bounding box will be chosen.

The structure of the YOLO algorithm is similar to the structure of the convolutional window algorithm:

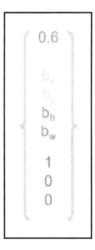

The first value is P_c, which is maybe 60% for the bounding box that lies at the left end of the screen, then we have the bounding box's properties, which are relative to the image, and then the class number. In a similar fashion, we can depict the structure for the other boxes.

There are certain windows that have a significant role, despite the fact that the P_c value is 0. This is because the YOLO algorithm believes that the windows that contain the center are the most important.

The YOLO algorithm uses this method for training and only the windows that contain the center will be optimized for the bounding boxes that have an object in it.

Max suppression and anchor boxes

Now we'll solve the problem of choosing the best bounding box from many such boxes generated during the testing time, and the challenge of when a window happens to own more than one bounding box center.

Max suppression

Although during training we assign only one bounding box to a window, the one that owned the center, during testing it can happen that many windows think that they have the center of the best bounding box.

For example, we may have three bounding boxes, and therefore three windows on the center of the bounding boxes, and each of these windows thinks that they have the best bounding box:

But what we'll need is only one bounding box, and preferably the best one. Max suspension will solve this problem.

The max suppression algorithm looks like this if written in observable code:

```
list = all bounding boxes

repeat until no boxes left in list
    maxBox=choose box with max Pc
    list.remove(maxBox)
      for box in list
          if(IoU(box, maxBox)>0.5)
              list.remove(box)
    showBox(maxBox);
```

Let's follow these steps to understand how max pooling resolves the bounding box problem:

1. Assign all the bounding boxes to a list.
2. Continue to repeat the previous code, as long as the list isn't empty.
3. Choose the bounding box with a maximum value of the P_c, or the probability that the selected pixels have a bounding box. In this case, if we look at the probabilities in the car image, the 94% windows, that bounding box will be the max box in the car image.
4. Remove the max box from the list.
5. For the remaining bounding boxes, such as the yellow one in the center of the car image and the bunch of boxes surrounding it, do the following:
    1. If any of the bounding boxes left shares more than 50% with a max box, remove it. And as we can see, the yellow box on the left hand bunch of boxes, with 74% probability, shares more than 50% with the max box, so we remove it.
    2. **Intersection over union** (**IOU**) divides the intersection areas with the union, for example, in the car image inside the 94% probability box, and if that's more than 50%, it means the two boxes—76% and 94%—share more than 50%. It removes that box from the list, so the yellow box of 76% will be removed.
    3. Choose the max box from the remaining boxes, and if the probabilities the max box is at 91%, we immediately remove the 90% box from the list.

4. Go through the remaining bunch of boxes and check whether any of them share more than 50%. Remove them both. We'll be left with these bounding boxes:

6. Now the list has only two bounding boxes. We choose the max again, which is 89%, remove the box it, then for the remaining boxes in the list, which is only the yellow box, we check to see if it shares more than 50% with the max box, which obviously it does, and therefore we remove the yellow box with 71% probability:

Now we check the list. The list is empty, and we have only three bounding boxes, and indeed they are the best bounding boxes with maximum probabilities.

Anchor boxes

This problem is related to the situation when a window owns several bounding boxes' centers.

As this screenshot shows here:

The bounding box represents the car, and the center of the bounding box represents a person. Looking at the structure we've seen so far, we can't solve this problem, because each of these windows has the following structure:

This structure can represent only one bounding box, so the windows in the screenshot can have either the car bounding box dimensions or the person ones, but not both.

And if we look at the grids for each of the windows, we have these structures:

$$8 \times 9 \times (5+C)$$
$$8 \times 9 \times 8$$

We're going to solve this problem by using different shapes of bounding boxes, which are called anchor boxes.

In this case, we choose two boxes: one the fits to a car shape and one that's a bit taller than it is wide, which fits to a person. For each of these anchor boxes, we use this structure:

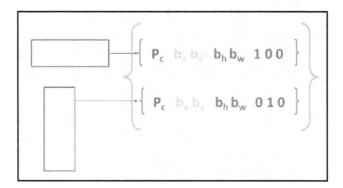

P_c is the bounding box properties and the class:

```
8 x 9 x 2 x (5+C)
8 x 9 x 16
```

Now, notice how the dimensions change:

```
8 x 9 x 2 x (5+C)
8 x 9 x 16
```

These will be the number of the anchor boxes. We've doubled the amount of information needed.

In the car and person picture, for example, the P_c for the anchor box surrounding the car would be 1, because we have an object with a rectangular shape. And the class will be 1 0 0 since this is a car.

Then we try for the shape of the bounding box surrounding the person: P_c will be 1, the bounding boxes properties will represent the list shape, and now we'll have 0 1 0, which represents the person.

In this way, by choosing different shapes, we're able to assign more information to a window, and a window basically can own many centers of the bounding boxes.

Building a real-time video, car, and pedestrian detection application

We'll use the YOLO algorithm to build a Java real-time object detection application. We'll use transfer learning to load the YOLO model that was trained on ImageNet and the COCO dataset. Among other objects, it is trying to detect cars, pedestrians, and traffic lights with quite high accuracy.

Architecture of the application

Before jumping into the code, let's see what the architecture of the application will look like:

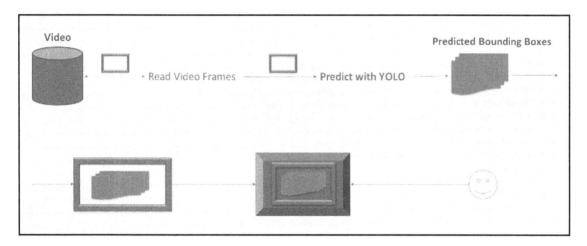

First, we read the video frames at a certain rate, maybe 30 frames per second. Then, we give each of the frames to the YOLO model, which gives us the bounding-box predictions for each of the objects. Once we have the bounding boxes' dimensions, which are relative to the window that owns the center, and the number of the grids together with the frame size, it's possible to precisely draw the bounding boxes in to the frame, as shown in the preceding diagram, for each of the objects. Then we simply show the modified frame with the bounding boxes to the user.

Now, if we have enough processing power, this architecture will work just fine, but when used with a CPU, it doesn't scale well. The reason is that even if YOLO is optimized and really fast, it won't work well with a low-power CPU. These steps take some time, from 300 milliseconds to 1.5 seconds, depending on the resolution of the frame and the grid size we choose. The user will be able to see one frame per 1.5 seconds, which doesn't look good—we'll have a slow-motion video. This would be the case only when used with CPU; on the other hand, when we use GPU, YOLO does a great job and provides real-time predictions, so this architecture will work just fine.

YOLO V2-optimized architecture

Let's see how we can somehow fix the problem by introducing another optimized architecture:

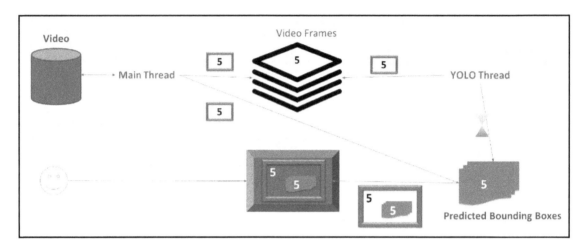

First, we will divide the execution into two independent parts. The main thread, or the video thread, which simply continues to read the frames, puts it on a stack and then shows those frames into the screen together if the bounding boxes exist. Then we have another thread, the YOLO thread, which is independent from the main thread; it reads those frames from the stack, and it produces bounding-box predictions. Since the YOLO thread, which is the slowest one, isn't mixing with the main thread, it isn't slowing down the thread that's showing the video. The flow of the frames will go normally, and in the screen, we'll see a high-quality video. Most of the time, this architecture will work just fine.

However, this isn't perfect. Let's see one example (please refer the optimized YOLO architecture image): suppose the sixth frame comes in and then the main thread will be put on the stack; this will show us the frame on the screen. It will first check for the bounding boxes.

Since the YOLO thread may take some time to produce the new bounding boxes for the sixth frame, it may be that the main thread will take all bounding boxes from the fifth frame, mix them together, draw the rectangles, and show those boxes on the screen, which will be the sixth frame with the fifth frame bounding boxes.

This works well if the video doesn't move or change frames too fast. If we have a fast-moving car, or maybe people running, it will show us outdated bounding boxes. The speed of the movement depends on the mode we choose, a function available in some graphical user interfaces. We could choose high resolution, which means that the YOLO thread will be slowed down, or we may choose a lower resolution and grid size, and that means that we will see almost a real-time into the screen.

Coding the application

Let's jump into the code.

First we have the class, the `VideoPlayer`:

```
public class VideoPlayer {

    private static final String AUTONOMOUS_DRIVING_RAMOK_TECH = "Autonomous
Driving(ramok.tech)";
    private String windowName;
    private volatile boolean stop = false;
    private Yolo yolo;
    private final OpenCVFrameConverter.ToMat converter = new
OpenCVFrameConverter.ToMat();
    public final static AtomicInteger atomicInteger = new AtomicInteger();


    public void startRealTimeVideoDetection(String videoFileName, Speed
selectedIndex, boolean yoloModel) throws java.lang.Exception {
        log.info("Start detecting video " + videoFileName);
        int id = atomicInteger.incrementAndGet();
        windowName = AUTONOMOUS_DRIVING_RAMOK_TECH + id;
        log.info(windowName);
        yolo = new Yolo(selectedIndex, yoloModel);
        startYoloThread();
        runVideoMainThread(videoFileName, converter);
    }
```

The YOLO thread which simply runs in the background and predicts these bounding boxes, so we have a pre-trained model YOLO here, which is loaded once the application starts, and then we produce the results and simply convert those to a list of predicted objects. The detected object contains the center of the bounding box, height, width, and information that helps in producing bounding boxes, and then we start the main thread, which is the video thread:

```
private void runVideoMainThread(String videoFileName,
OpenCVFrameConverter.ToMat toMat) throws FrameGrabber.Exception {
```

```
        FFmpegFrameGrabber grabber = initFrameGrabber(videoFileName);
        while (!stop) {
            Frame frame = grabber.grab();
            if (frame == null) {
                log.info("Stopping");
                stop();
                break;
            }
            if (frame.image == null) {
                continue;
            }
            yolo.push(frame);
            opencv_core.Mat mat = toMat.convert(frame);
            yolo.drawBoundingBoxesRectangles(frame, mat);
            imshow(windowName, mat);
            char key = (char) waitKey(20);
            // Exit this loop on escape:
            if (key == 27) {
                stop();
                break;
            }
        }
    }
}
```

This thread grabs the frames from the video file and then it puts those frames into a stack so the YOLO thread can read them, and then it draws those rectangles, which contain the low-level details, if we have the information of the detected object, the grid size, we can basically draw those into the frame, so it mixes the frame with the bounding boxes. Finally, we show this modified frame to the user.

We can choose three modes through the graphical user interface, fast, medium, and slow:

```
public enum Speed {

    FAST("Real-Time but low accuracy", 224, 224, 7, 7),
    MEDIUM("Almost Real-time and medium accuracy", 416, 416, 13, 13),
    SLOW("Slowest but high accuracy", 608, 608, 19, 19);

    private final String name;

    public final int width;
    public final int height;
    public final int gridWidth;
    public final int gridHeight;

    public String getName() {
        return name;
    }
}
```

```
    Speed(String name, int width, int height, int gridWidth, int
gridHeight) {

        this.name = name;
        this.width = width;
        this.height = height;
        this.gridWidth = gridWidth;
        this.gridHeight = gridHeight;
    }

    @Override
    public String toString() {
        return name;
    }
}
```

The fastest one has a low resolution and a 7 x 7 grid size, which is very small. This will be fast, so you have almost real-time bounding boxes, basically we may not detect everything in the image.

As we move to the medium and the slow, we increase the resolution, and we also double the grid size, from 7 to 7 to 13 by 13, and then, for slow, we had six more, 19 by 19. We will be able, for example, for the slowest one, to detect almost everything in the video, but actually the bounding box will be quite outdated. If we choose the slowest one, it will take more than two seconds to predict for one frame, so the bounding boxes we see are from two seconds in the past.

Let's see how the application will look:

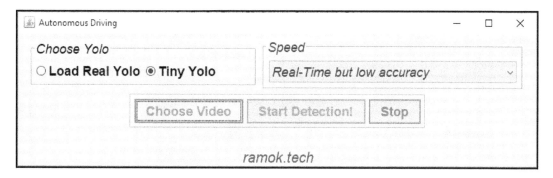

Let's choose the first video. For this one, we'll use the fastest one, **real time but lower accuracy**. Let's see how that looks:

We're able to detect the cars as they come in, but we may miss some things, such as some of the cars and some of the people.

Next, let's look at a slow YOLO, with twice the resolution and a 13x13 grid. Let's see what happens:

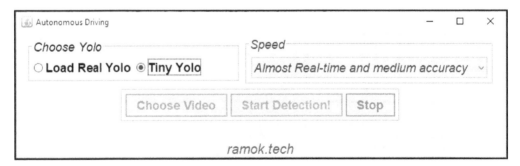

As we can see, we have more bounding boxes here:

We detected the person a bit late but there are more cars, which means more bounding boxes.

The traffic light comes a bit late, but we were able to see it:

If we choose the third option, we'll see more bounding boxes, but the response will be rather slow.

Let's try to run another one having a medium amount of frames. As we can see, this bounding box is is quite delayed:

Let's choose the fastest option. So now, as we can see, we detect a bit faster, and the bounding boxes are a bit more frequent:

The algorithm does a good job here. That's it for the demo, and considering that we have just CPU processing power, actually the results are quite good. If were to use the sliding window solution, we wouldn't be able to obtain such a good output.

Summary

In this chapter, we learned about the object localization problem, as well as how to label the data along and modify the network layer of the neural network to fit this problem. We detected objects using the sliding window solution and the convolutional window technique. Lastly, we delved into the state-of-the-art YOLO algorithm, that overcomes all the downsides of the older techniques.

In the next chapter, we'll create art with a neural style transfer.

5
Creating Art with Neural Style Transfer

In this chapter, we will be exploring the convolution neural network internals by visualizing what these layers are trying to learn. Then, we will look at the neural style transfer problem, and how to solve that problem by using the knowledge about the layers learning process. We will then continue with a content cost function intuition, together with a bit more formal mathematical definition of the cost and derivation. We will go through the details of building the style cost function, which are slightly more complex, and how to efficiently capture the style of an image in terms of convolution layers. Finally, we will present the optimized architecture, together with the core details for the Java implementation for neural style transfer. We will also show an image sample for a few iterations.

We will be covering the following topics:

- What are convolution network layers learning
- Neural style transfer
- Applying content cost function
- Applying style cost function
- Building a neural network that produces art

What are convolution network layers learning?

In this section, we will explore what the convolution layers are doing while learning. Understanding what activation layers are learning will not only help us to generate art, but will provide us with some useful insight that gives us greater opportunities for improvements.

First, we will see how to visualize the layers' knowledge, using the paper from Zeiler and Fergus 2013, which really does a great job in revealing what the layers are learning. Then we will look at a few examples from the same paper.

Let's look at the VGG-16 architecture, which we have studied previously in Chapter 3, *Transfer Learning and Deep CNN Architectures,* which has several convolution layers followed by fully connected layers and a softmax layer:

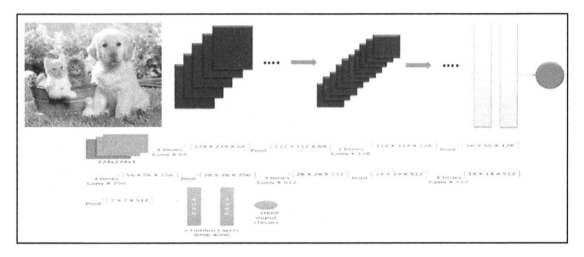

To train the model, we have to pick one of the layers, let's consider the second convolutional layer. We will monitor the activation values of 9,000 units or neurons. So, we may choose any of these nine units from the neurons. When the training is complete, we will choose only nine maximum values produced by the nine chosen neurons, together with the image patch that originally caused those neurons to fire maximum values.

So for example, if we have chosen the unit (the dog's nose) as shown in the following diagram, then it may happen that only this part of the image caused that neuron to fire the maximum value:

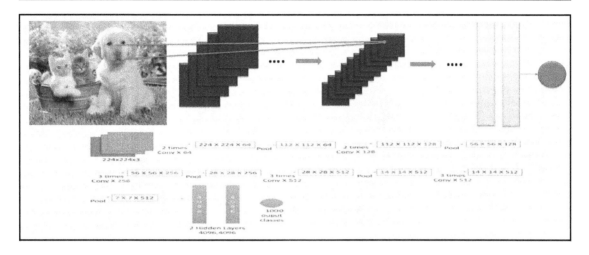

Whereas for the other neuron, the part of the cat causes the network to fire maximum values:

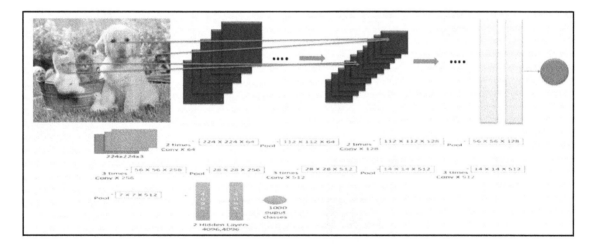

Next, perhaps the bottom most neuron is more interested in the grass and fires maximum values as shown in the diagram, while the other part of the photo has minimum values:

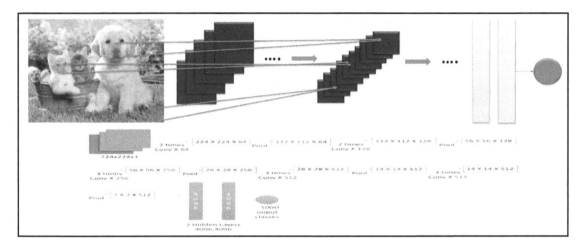

In short, the part of the image that fires maximum neurons activation values is just visualized. Although this looks simple in a high-level description, the reality is that it's a bit more of a sophisticated method using the convolution layers, and then moving back from the convolution layer to the image.

Let's see some more examples from the table to gain a more consistent idea of what layers are learning as we go deeper into the network.

So, if we visualize the first layer, we can see that the first neuron is interested in diagonal lines as shown in the following diagram:

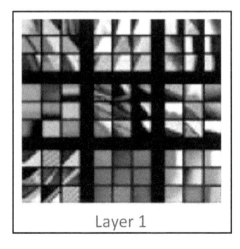

Layer 1

For the third and the fourth part of the **Layer 1**, we'll see more vertical lines and horizontal lines detected by the neurons, and the eighth part is kind of obsessed with a green color. It is noticeable that all these are really small parts of the original image, and the layer is catching low-level features.

Let's go to the second layer:

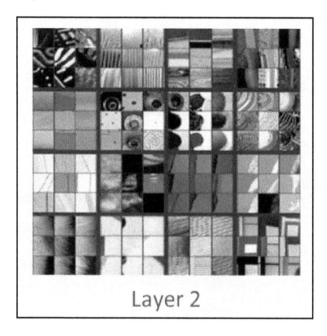

Layer 2

The neurons of this layer start to detect a number of additional features. The sixth and the seventh neurons start capturing round shapes, while the fourteenth one is obsessed with a yellow color.

At the third layer, the neuron starts to detect more interesting stuff. The sixth neuron is more interested in round shapes that look such as tires, the tenth one, it's kind of difficult to say, appears to be more interested in round shapes that are an orange color, while by the eleventh neuron, we see that it is recognizing humans already:

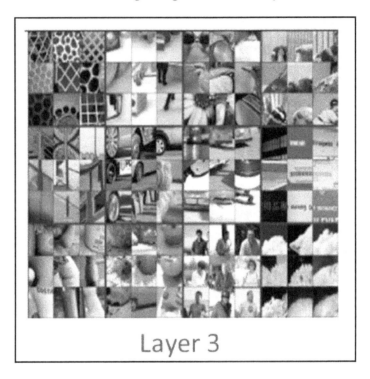

Let's delve a bit deeper at the fourth and fifth layers:

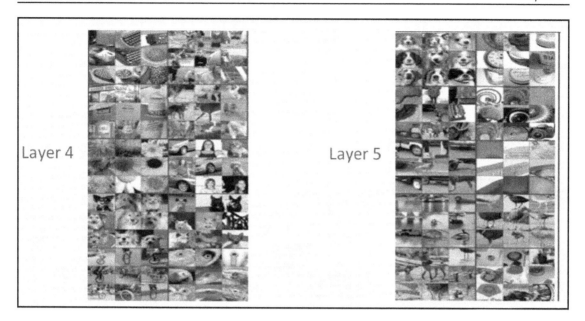

From the preceding diagram, you can see that as we go deeper into the layers, the neurons capture the bigger part of the images, therefore, capturing high-level features of the images, as compared to the low-level layers that capture the smaller part of the image. We can see from the preceding image that the first neuron of the fifth layer is already into dogs, while in the fourth layer we have keyboards, dogs, bicycles, and so on.

Let's summarize our findings. The early layers of a neural network are learning low-level features, such as symbol lines and shapes, whereas when we go deeper, we see that the layers on top are learning more complex features, such as detecting humans, animals, cars, and trees.

In the next section, we will use this intuition and knowledge to generate art from images using neural style transfer.

Neural style transfer

In this section, we are going to learn what neural style transfer is, the cost function, and what we are trying to minimize in the case of neural style transfer. When we are referring to style transfer, we will always have a content image followed by a style image, or the artwork, and what we want to do is to have a final image that looks such as the content image, but painted with a style from the styled image. Basically it's like the style is being transferred from the Van Gogh picture (as shown in the following diagram) to the content image:

Let's consider another example which is shown as follows. We have the content image once again, then we have the style image or the artwork, and we have a final, or the third image that looks like similar to both of those previous images, but in the same way they also look somewhat different:

In a few words, this is the application we will try to build in this section. We take two images and generate a third one that looks kind of similar to both of them.

As we have seen so far, neural networks are updating weights. With each update the model prediction or the hypothesis comes closer to the real data. So, we have the cost function measuring how similar the hypothesis is to the real data by calculating the square difference between them.

Ideally, we want the cost function to be zero, because that simply means that the hypothesis is exactly the same as the real data. The following formula is used to calculate the cost function of the hypothesis data:

$$J=1/m*sum(H(w)-Y)^2 \text{-Cost function}$$

The neural network does a really good job of predicting the same hypothesis as the real data. In the case of neural style transfer, we want the same, but with only one difference; instead of having only one ground truth, we have two of them. So we have two cost functions, one that measures the difference between the contact image and the generated image, and the second one, which measures the difference between the style image and the generated image. Ideally, we want these two cost functions to still be as low as possible, because that will mean that our generated image is similar to the content image and style image at the same time.

These coefficients, the alpha and the beta, simply impact how similar we want the generated image to be to the content or style image. So in a few words, if we have alpha to be way bigger than beta, that means that our generated image will be more similar to the content image rather than the style image. So these are just weights impacting how similar you want the generated image to be with a content or the style image.

Minimizing the cost function

Our first step will be to generate a noisy random image (G) that looks a bit like the content image (**C**). The following example on the right is maybe 80% noisy random and it looks 20% like the content image:

Also, we can generate a pure noisy image, and it will work just fine, but it speeds up a bit if we start with a more content-like image. Then, we will use gradient descent (*J(G)*) exactly as we saw in the first section, and use the following formula:

$$J(G) = \alpha * J(C, G) + \beta * J(S, G)$$

$$G = G - \frac{dJ(G)}{dG}$$

We will use the feedback, which is the derivation of the cost function, to update the weights. Now, instead of updating the weights, we will additionally update the image's pixels. Here, the *G* is referring to the pixels of the generated image. And iteration by iteration, the generated image will change to look more like the content and the style image, because the cost function actually measures the difference between the content and generated image, and the style and the generated image. So maybe after 10 iterations the image will appears as follows:

After 100 iterations, it will appear as follows:

And after 200 iterations, it will appear as follows:

After 500, we see that the image generated from a noisy image looks more similar to the content and the style image at the same time, which is shown as follows:

This is happening because we use the feedback of two cost functions—one that measures the difference between the generated image and the content, and the second one that measures the difference between the generated image and the style one. The feedback that we receive is used to update the pixels of that generated image so that it comes closer to the cost function, and indirectly, closer to these images. Cost and style functions are absolutely essential for the quality of generated images, since they are the only feedback we used to update pixels iteration by iteration. In the next section, we will use the knowledge acquired in the previous section about what the layers were learning, to build up those functions. More specifically, we will start with a content cost function.

Applying content cost function

In this section, we are going to define the content cost function and then formalize the function a bit more by calculating the derivative, which we will use for further applications as well. We will use transfer learning or a pre-trained convolution architecture, such as VGG-16, but this time in a different way. Instead of using the model for this prediction for the softmax layer, we will use the layer's knowledge or their ability to capture the features of the images as depicted in the following diagram:

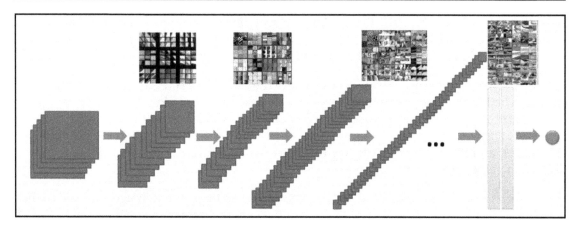

As we saw in the first section, *What are convolution network layers learning,* the first layers of the neural network capture rather low-level features, such as shapes or maybe colors, and as we move deeper, the layers are detecting more high-level features, and at the same time also capture a bigger part of the image, as shown in the preceding diagram.

Suppose that we feed our content and generated image to this neural network, and for each of them, we store the corresponding activation values as well, as shown in the following diagram:

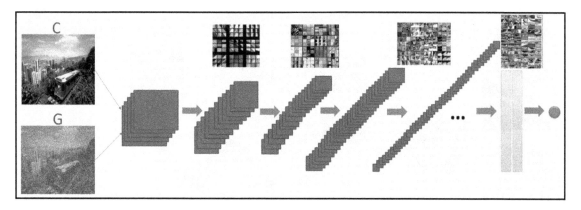

A pre-trained network, such as VGG-16 was trained for a long time with millions of images, so these layers of the network have really learned to capture a vast, complex set of features during that time.

Now, knowing this, if the activation values of a specific layer between those two images are quite similar, then we can say that the images are also similar. In some way, this is true, but of course that highly depends on the layer as well.

For early layers, even those activation values are the same between the images. We can't predict whether the images are the same, since those capture only low-level features. So basically, even if some images share their shapes and some colors, it does not make them similar. But as we go deeper, the layers detect more high-level features and bigger parts of the images, and that's when we can say that those two images are the same, where the activation values are also the same.

Remember, we want the generated image to be similar to the content image, but also to the style image at the same time. So we don't want the generated image to be identical to the content image, but in a way, we need to leave some room also for the style image as well. So, it is not in our best interest to go on the deepest layer of this neural network, because that will make this generated image identical to the content image. We need the end, but not very deep into it.

So in our example here, this layer could be okay. So, we will take the activation in the layer l for the content and generated image, and depending on the comparison as to how similar or how different they are, we will use that feedback to update the pixels of the generated image to be more similar to the content image. But again we'll leave room here also for the style image, and that's why we won't go that deep:

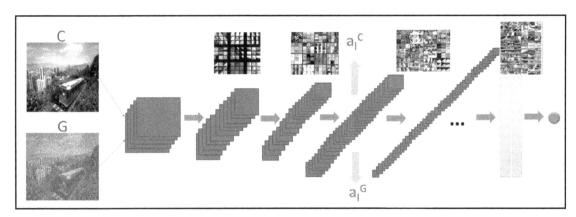

Let's try to formalize a bit further. So, we had this general cost function formula:

$$J(G) = \alpha * J(C, G) + \beta * J(S, G)$$

This is simply the sum of the content cost function and the style cost function, which we will see in the next section. And this coefficient simply affects how similar you want the generated image to be to one of these.

So, the cost function of the content image will look like this, where, 1/4 is multiplied by the width, height, and the number of channels in the layer that we choose to compare:

$$J(C, G) = \frac{1}{4 * W * H * C} * \left\| a_l^C - a_l^G \right\|^2$$

And as we go deeper, the width and the height tend to shrink, while the number of channels increases. And then we have the squared difference between those activation values of the content and generated image, and this is quite similar to what we have seen so far.

Now, the cost function itself will tell us how similar those two activation values are between them, but actually, in order to change the pixels and the weights, we need to turn this into a feedback, and mathematically that is done by the derivative of the cost function. And in this instance, it is quite simple. So we just used simple algebra and put two at the front, and 2 x 4 makes two, and we leave this unchanged because those are just constants, and then this ends up just being the absolute difference between the activation values:

$$\frac{dJ(C, G)}{dG} = \frac{1}{2 * W * H * C} * \left\| a_l^C - a_l^G \right\|$$

So each time we will use this derivative, and of course the derivative of the style cost function as well, to update the pixels of the image to look more similar in this case to the content image. In the next section, we will also see the style cost function.

Applying style cost function

In this section, we are going to see what is the style in terms of convolution layers, and then based on that intuition, we'll build the style cost function. In the end, we'll go through a slightly more formal definition of the style cost function.

How to capture the style

A part of the process is quite similar to what we have seen in the content cost function. So, we will still use convolution layers to capture image features and we will feed the neural network with a generated image, and then instead of the content image, we will use the style image here. And once we do that, we have the features captured for each of the layers.

Let's suppose that we pick up this layer as a feature detector, and for the sake of simplicity, let's suppose that layer has only four channels in comparison to many such channels in real convolution architectures, as shown in the following diagram:

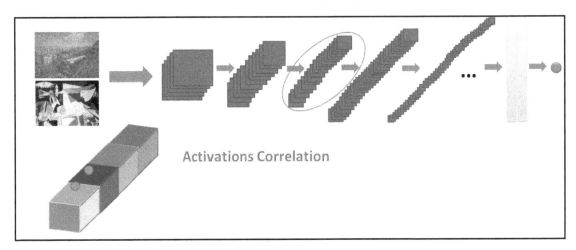

The style on the second layer will be defined as the activation correlation between channels. But, what that means is that we will have a look at the activation numbers between channels, their degree of correlation, and in some way, how similar they are when together. And of course, we have many such activations in one channel. For instance, for the first channel we'll have a look at each of the activations on the first channel, how similar they are with the activation numbers on each of those activation numbers on the second channel, and then we will do the same for the first channel activation numbers and third channel activation numbers, their degree of correlation, and with a four channel as well.

Now, we will repeat the same process, but starting from the second channel. So, we will see how correlated the activation numbers are with the first channel activation numbers, and then with a third, and then with the fourth. And that gives us the correlation between the second channel and all other channels on this layer. Although the process may be clearer, still one question remains; why does this represents the style? So why is this correlation the style after all?

Let's suppose that we had the feature-detecting for the layer that is shown in the following image:

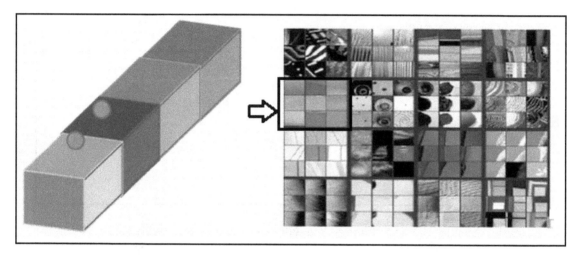

For those two activations, let's assume that they detect the vertical line, and the other one the orange (the highlighted square) color. If they are highly correlated, that means that whenever a vertical line is encountered, the orange color is also present. So they always tend to occur together.

On the other hand, if they are not correlated, it would mean that whenever a vertical line is encountered, most probably there will be no orange color around then. In a few words, the correlation enables us to capture the degree, or the level of the feature combinations together. In contrast to the cost function, we are not going to compare the activations directly, but instead, the activation correlations, because those are detecting the style of the role.

Style cost function

Let's see how to get the correlations once you have the activations. Correlation will be calculated simply as the multiplication between the numbers of the activations. If the result is high, the multiplication result is high, then we say that those two activations are correlated together. Otherwise, if they are different and the multiplication has a low result, then they aren't correlated together. Since channels are feature detectors, we are more interested in channel correlation rather than some specific activations. So we are going to multiply all the activations between two channels, and then we'll sum up to get some value as shown in the following image, and that value will tell us the degree of correlation between those two channels are:

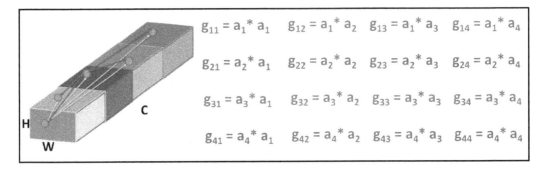

For example, consider the first channel. We will multiply all the activations here with the second channel activation, and then total them. That will give us this small g_{12}, which is simply the degree of correlation degree between the first channel and the second channel. And we continue to do the same with a third channel, and with a fourth channel, so these g_{13} and g_{14}, respectively provide us the degree of correlation degree between the first channel, and the third one, and with a fourth. Then the process starts all over again, but now from the second channel. So, we will multiply all the activation values with a first channel and then total them to produce this g_{21}, which simply is the correlation between the second channel and the first one. And we will do the same for the other one, so this g_{24} is in correlation between the second and fourth channel.

Then the process starts from the third channel, and the corresponding row gives us a correlation of the third channel with all other channels, and the fourth channel with all these three channels as well. Now observe this kind of diagonal here, g_{11}, g_{22}, g_{33}, and g_{44}. We are calculating the correlation within the same channel. The reason we do that is because activation correlation within the same channel measures how big this channel feature is. Hence, the feature that the channel is capturing, impacts the image as a whole, and we also understand the popularity of the feature in the image, that is being detected by the channel.

For instance, if a channel correlation with itself is high, for example, the g_{33} is high, and the channel captures horizontal lines, this means that the image has a lot of horizontal lines. So this operation is quite useful because it is capturing the style in the image as a whole, , in other words, the popularity of a feature detected by your channel throughout the image as a whole. As we know, due to performance reasons, neural network operations are done through matrixes. Therefore the correlation is a matrix, called the gram matrix, or the style matrix.

Let's see how the gram matrix is calculated:

First we will need to turn the preceding three dimensional structure into a two dimensional structure. We do that by simply putting every value in the first channel, which is two dimensional, in a row, and then we do the same for other channels as well. So, each of the rows represents the activation values in each of the channels. Next, we will simply multiply the matrix with itself, but in its transpose form.

So we turn rows into columns. Then, according to the multiplication of matrix's rules, we will have the first row activations multiplied each with the first column, and then sum up to get the first cell value, which basically is the g_{11}, so the correlation of this layer with itself. And then for the next cell, we have to multiply the first row with a second column, and then sum up, which gives us g_{12}, because this first row represents the first channel, and this second column basically represents the second channel, so this d_{12} is exactly the correlation between the first channel and the second one. And then we do the same for the other rows and columns. For example, the third row will be multiplied with the second column at some point, and then gives us simply this g_{32}, which is the correlation between the third channel and the second channel, because the second column is just the second channel activations. In the end, we gain this gram matrix in a very performant way, so it is really fast, because each of these correlations can be done in parallel, thanks to the matrices.

Ultimately, what we will do is simply compare the gram matrices of style image and generated image together, and what we want is fir those gram matrices to be as similar as possible; since they are capturing the style, a close similarity would mean that the generated image and the style image are sharing almost the same style:

$$compare\ g_l^S\ with\ g_l^G \qquad g = c\ \cdot\ H \cdot W \quad compare\ g_l^S\ with\ g_l^G \quad = \quad \begin{matrix} g_{11} & g_{12} & g_{13} & g_{14} \\ g_{21} & g_{22} & g_{23} & g_{24} \\ g_{31} & g_{32} & g_{33} & g_{34} \\ g_{41} & g_{42} & g_{43} & g_{44} \end{matrix}$$

Let's see more formally how that is done. First, we have the general cost function, we have already seen:

$$J(G) = \alpha * J(C, G) + \beta * J(S, G)$$

Now let's see the style cost function. And it is being defined such as this: 1/4 and then multiplied by the squared dimensions of the layer we pick up first. And in a moment, we will see why this is squared in the style cost function. Then we multiply by the squared difference of the gram matrices as shown in the following formula:

$$J(S, G) = \frac{1}{4 * (W * H * C)^2} * \left\| g_l^S - g_l^G \right\|^2$$

This is quite similar to what we have seen in the content cost function, but instead of having activations here we simply have the gram matrix:

$$g = a_l * a_l^T;\ dg = 2 * a_l^T$$

As you will recall from the previous section, the gram matrix is being defined as deactivation multiplied by the activation the same, but transposed. So if we think of this as just the square of the activation, then the derivative will be two, multiplied by the activation transposed. And this also explains why we squared the layers' dimensions; we don't have just one activation here, but we have two activations, the same activation multiplied by itself. We therefore need to multiply the *d* measures by themselves as well, in order to have everything consistent.

Since the activation is multiplied with itself we need to also multiply the dimensions. Now the cost function gives us just a hint of how similar those two gram matrices are, or how similar the style of those two images are. In order to turn that into a feedback to cause those images to come together more closely, we need the derivation of the cost function. The cost function is calculated as follows:

$$\frac{dJ(S,G)}{dG} = \frac{1}{(W * H * C)^2} * \left\| g_i^S - g_i^G \right\| * (a_i^G)^T$$

As we can see in the preceding formula, one divided by the squared of dimensions does not change because it is just a constant. Then this force goes away because the two that comes from the derivation of the gram matrix is multiplied by the other two here, which comes in front. Then, 4 x 4 gives us one, then new multiplication of the simple difference between the gram matrices. In comparison to the content cost function, we have an additional term, which is basically the transpose of the activation that comes from the derivation of the gram matrix, where two is multiplied by the transpose activation. There is one final detail pertaining to the style cost function; we are going to use several layers' feedback instead of just one, as we will see in the following section, when we will build a neural network that produces art.

Building a neural network that produces art

In this section, we are going to build a Java application for creating art. Before jumping into the code and application, let's look at the high-level description on how is it implemented. We will use transfer learning with the pre-trained VGG-16 architecture, trained on ImageNet dataset, which is a bunch of convolution layers in the following diagram:

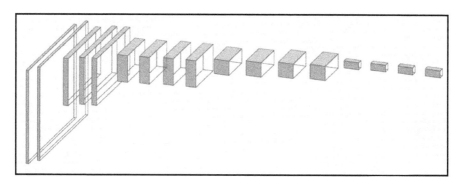

Basically, as we go deeper, the depth of the third dimension increases, while the first two dimensions shrink in time.

At first, we are going to fit a content image as an input through a forward pass as shown in the following diagram. Then, we will gain the values of all activation layers along with the prediction. But for neural style transfer, we are not interested in the prediction, but only in the activation layers, because those layers are capturing the image features. The following image depicts this clearly:

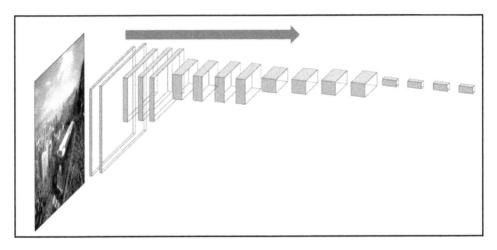

In the case of the content image, we are going to select one layer, which is shown in the following diagram, and register the activation values. This port denotes the fact that we are on the fourth group, as we can see in this case. We have five groups, as shown in the following image:

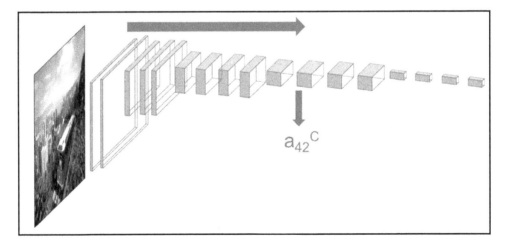

So there are five groups that are highlighted in the following diagram. We will select the second layer from the fourth convolution layers' group. Then, we are going to feed this style image and similarly, through a forward pass, we are going to gain all the activation layers. But instead of selecting only one, we will select multiple of them:

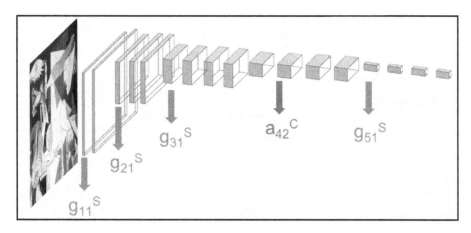

Another difference is that, instead of using the activation directly, we will transform those activations into gram matrices. The reason we do that, as we learned in the previous section, is because the gram matrices capture the style better than the activations directly. And those grams are g_{11}s, g_{21}s, g_{31}s, g_{51}s, as shown in the following diagram. Then finally the generated image is fed to gram matrices, which at the beginning looks a bit noisy, as shown in the following diagram:

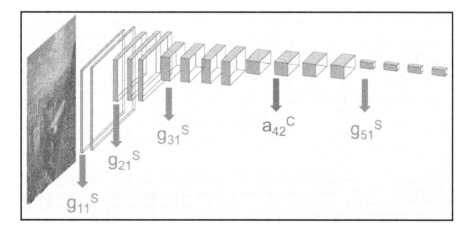

Similarly, through a forward pass, we are going to get all the gram matrices and the activations for the content selected layers:

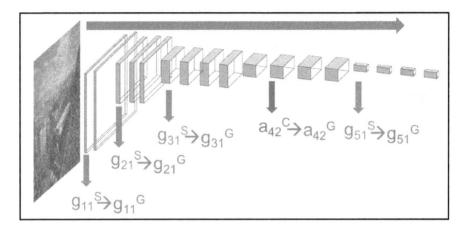

Now, we will calculate the difference by means of the cost function, and then use that feedback for the derivation to go through the back propagation till the generated image, to change it to look a bit more like content or maybe the style.

So basically, if we take this g_{51} here, first we will calculate the difference, then the derivation to use that feedback, and after that, we are going back, step by step to the generated image, and change it a bit to look more like the style image. Similarly, for the content layer, we are doing the cost function as we saw, then the derivation of it, and after we do the derivation, we are ready to go through a back propagation till the generated image, to change to look a bit more like the content image.

We repeat the same for the three other style layers. And after that, the generated image may look a bit more like the style and the content image. If we are not satisfied with the result, we can simply repeat the same process. A forward pass only calculates the functions, that are marked by the red arrow in the preceding diagram, and also calculates the activation of the red and gram matrices. The green and the blue functions are not calculated again, because the content image and the style image did not change, so those are stored in memory and received as feedback relatively more quickly.

We repeat this process until we are satisfied with the result. So each time, we have a new generated image, which is generated through a forward pass, different activation, and gram matrices. This is basically the fundamental concept behind the working code. Let's put this all together slightly more formal manner.

We have the total cost function, defined as the content cost function and multiple style cost functions. And also, we have the alpha and the beta, which simply impact or control how much you want the generated image to look like the content or the style image. The following formula relates to the total cost function:

$$J(G) = \alpha * J(C, G) + \beta * (k1 * J(S, G)^{l1} + k2 * J(S, G)^{l2} + k3 * J(S, G)^{l3} + k4 * J(S, G)^{l4})$$

The content cost function is simply the squared difference between the activations in a selected layer, while the cost function on the style is the squared difference of the gram matrices, rather than activations directly. The first formula reflects the content cost function, while the second formula is the cost function on the styled image:

$$J(C, G) = \frac{1}{4 * W * H * C} * \left\| a_i^C - a_i^G \right\|^2$$

$$J(S, G) = \frac{1}{4 * (W * H * C)^2} * \left\| g_i^S - g_i^G \right\|^2$$

Let's see how the code looks.

First, we need to select the style layers, and here, we have five of those style layers; on the left is the name of the style layer on VGG-16 architecture, while on the right we have the coefficient:

```
public class NeuralStyleTransfer {

    public static final String[] STYLE_LAYERS = new String[]{
            "block1_conv1,0.5",
            "block2_conv1,1.0",
            "block3_conv1,1.5",
            "block4_conv2,3.0",
            "block5_conv1,4.0"
    };
```

And here, along the lines of what we have mentioned previously, the deeper layers are contributing more to the style in comparison to the low level layers, but we also want these early layers in the play, because they may have some low-level details, such as color capturing, which are quite interesting for this style. That's why we use multiple layers in here. But it will be quite interesting to change those weights and to see how the generated image will be different. Then we have the content layer name, which is a `block4_conv2`. Now once we get all the feedback from the style layers and this content layer, we need to update the image:

```
private static final String CONTENT_LAYER_NAME = "block4_conv2";
    /**
     * ADAM
     * Possible values 0.8-0.95
     */
    private static final double BETA_MOMENTUM = 0.9;
    /**
     * ADAM
     * Below values rarely change
     */
    private static final double BETA2_MOMENTUM = 0.999;
    private static final double EPSILON = 0.00000008;
```

The way we update the generated image each time is by means of an automatic updater, because it is quite optimized, and it has these three parameters as shown in the preceding code. Then we have the alpha and the beta; alpha represents the degree to which you want the generated image to look like the content, while the beta represents the degree to which we want the generated image to look like the style image:

```
public static final double ALPHA = 5;
    public static final double BETA = 100;

    private static final double LEARNING_RATE = 2;
    private static final int ITERATIONS = 1000;
    /**
     * Higher resolution brings better results but
     * changing behind 300x400 on CPU become almost not computable and slow
     */
    public static final int HEIGHT = 224;
    public static final int WIDTH = 224;
    public static final int CHANNELS = 3;

    private ExecutorService executorService;
```

Beta is much bigger compared with the content image coefficient because, if you remember, we start with a noisy image that looks a bit like the content; that's why we need to make up the difference here to have the style impact greater so to catch up with the content image. Then we have the learning rate and iteration, which are already familiar, then the resolution of the image, and also the height, width, and channels. This is quite important; increasing the height and the width definitely shows a better generated image, so the quality is higher, but on CPU, I would suggest to not go behind this 300 x 400, or even 300 x 300, because then, it is difficult to compute. With GPU, of course, we can go to higher numbers such as 800, 900, with no concern.

Then we have the classes that handle the low-level details of the derivation, the cost function, and the image utilities, which we'll see in the following code:

```
final ImageUtilities imageUtilities = new ImageUtilities();
    private final ContentCostFunction contentCostFunction = new
ContentCostFunction();
    private final StyleCostFunction styleCostFunction = new
StyleCostFunction();

    public static void main(String[] args) throws Exception {
        new NeuralStyleTransfer().transferStyle();
    }

    public void transferStyle() throws Exception {

        ComputationGraph vgg16FineTune =
ramo.klevis.transfer.style.neural.VGG16.loadModel();

        INDArray content =
imageUtilities.loadImage(ImageUtilities.CONTENT_FILE);
        INDArray style =
imageUtilities.loadImage(ImageUtilities.STYLE_FILE);
        INDArray generated = imageUtilities.createGeneratedImage();

        Map<String, INDArray> contentActivationsMap =
vgg16FineTune.feedForward(content, true);
        Map<String, INDArray> styleActivationsMap =
vgg16FineTune.feedForward(style, true);
        HashMap<String, INDArray> styleActivationsGramMap =
buildStyleGramValues(styleActivationsMap);

        AdamUpdater adamUpdater = createADAMUpdater();
        executorService = Executors.newCachedThreadPool();

        for (int iteration = 0; iteration < ITERATIONS; iteration++) {
            long start = System.currentTimeMillis();
            //log.info("iteration " + iteration);
```

```
        CountDownLatch countDownLatch = new CountDownLatch(2);

        //activations of the generated image
        Map<String, INDArray> generatedActivationsMap =
vgg16FineTune.feedForward(generated, true);

        final INDArray[] styleBackProb = new INDArray[1];
        executorService.execute(() -> {
            try {
                styleBackProb[0] = backPropagateStyles(vgg16FineTune,
styleActivationsGramMap, generatedActivationsMap);
                countDownLatch.countDown();
            } catch (Exception e) {
                throw new RuntimeException(e);
            }
        });
        final INDArray[] backPropContent = new INDArray[1];
        executorService.execute(() -> {
            backPropContent[0] = backPropagateContent(vgg16FineTune,
contentActivationsMap, generatedActivationsMap);
            countDownLatch.countDown();
        });

        countDownLatch.await();
        INDArray backPropAllValues =
backPropContent[0].muli(ALPHA).addi(styleBackProb[0].muli(BETA));
        adamUpdater.applyUpdater(backPropAllValues, iteration);
        generated.subi(backPropAllValues.get());

        System.out.println((System.currentTimeMillis()) - start);
// log.info("Total Loss: " + totalLoss(styleActivationsMap,
generatedActivationsMap, contentActivationsMap));
        if (iteration % ImageUtilities.SAVE_IMAGE_CHECKPOINT == 0) {
            //save image can be found at
target/classes/styletransfer/out
            imageUtilities.saveImage(generated.dup(), iteration);
        }
    }

}
```

The following are the steps for obtaining the generated output image:

1. First we load the VGG-16 model through pre-trained `ImageNet`, as we saw when utilizing transfer learning
2. Then we load the content file through an image preprocessor, which handles the low-level details such as the scaling of the image down to the selected width and height we choose, and the image normalization
3. We also do the same here for this style, and then we have the generated image

Here is the output:

```
"C:\Program Files\Java\jdk-11.0.2\bin\java.exe" ...
[2019-02-06 17:51:30]Loaded [CpuBackend] backend
[2019-02-06 17:51:30]given scan urls are empty. set urls in the configuration
[2019-02-06 17:51:30]Number of threads used for NativeOps: 4
[2019-02-06 17:51:30]Reflections took 47 ms to scan 13 urls, producing 31 keys and 227 values
[2019-02-06 17:51:30]Number of threads used for BLAS: 4
[2019-02-06 17:51:30]Backend used: [CPU]; OS: [Windows 10]
[2019-02-06 17:51:30]Cores: [8]; Memory: [4.0GB];
[2019-02-06 17:51:30]Blas vendor: [OPENBLAS]
[2019-02-06 17:51:31]Downloading model to C:\Users\Admin\.deeplearning4j\vgg16_dl4j_inference.zip
```

As we mentioned, the generated image is partially similar to the content image and partially has some noise. In this example, we are using only 20% noise. The reason being, if you make your generated image look such as the content image, then you will get better and faster results. But even if you put 90% noise and 10% content image, eventually, you get the same result, but it may take longer for you to see the result.

That's why I will suggest starting with the lower noise if you want to see how the algorithm works first.

Then we need to calculate the activations for the content and restyle. So we will do the feed-forward process for the content image, and then for the style image.

For this style, we have another step; we need to gain the gram matrices because we are not using these activations directly. That's why we have built style gram values. Notice that these functions are kept in the memory, and not included in the iteration. So we will just use these values once they are executed for the first time. Then we create the ADAM update, and this executor service that optimizes the code for parallel processing. Basically, this code is already contributed to the deep learning community, but the version here at Packt Pub is quite optimized to run in parallel, and at the same time, we have some modifications in the VGG-16 model to produce better results.

So we are going forward to gain all the activations for the generated image, and then it's time to calculate the derivation, and then back propagate. Now this back propagation from the style layers and only content layers are going to be done in parallel, so for the style, we start another thread here, then for each of the layers, we start another thread, so we are going back and as we can see, the first step is to calculate the derivation of the cost function. Then this feedback is back propagated till the image. The same is also done for the content layer, so we back propagate till the first layer. And then the feedback that has been received, it's multiplied with the coefficient, then goes through the ADAM updater, and then finally the generated image is altered.

So the next time, if the image is different, we will go through the same process of the feed-forward, acquire all the activations, and then undertake this parallel processing, it will gain all the feedback to the back propagation.

Now, I would suggest to turn on the function if you want to debug how the cost function goes down or up step by step. Now, running the code really takes a long time, so gaining good result is starting from the 500 iterations, and to have 500 of iterations in a CPU, it takes something like three or four hours, so basically, it will take a long time to show the results in here; that's why I pre-run the application for just 45 iteration, and see how that looks like. So let's suppose that we use the following image as style image:

And the following as the content image:

Then let's see what the algorithm produces. For iterations 10, 15, 20, 25, 30, 35, 40, and 45, it is as shown in the following image. So after 45 iterations, the algorithm gives the content image as the output. So, basically after the 45th iteration, the generated image starts to obtain some color that is similar to the content image:

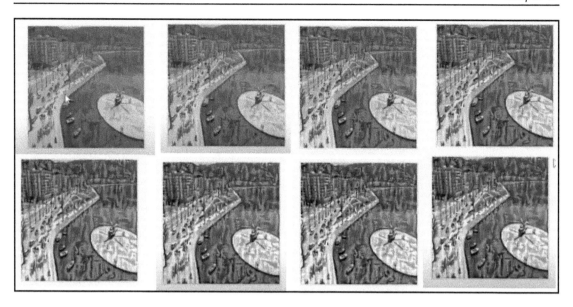

So we can see those colors in here, and after 500 and 1,000 duration, this will look more similar to the style and the content image in the same time. Basically, this was all about the application, and in the next section, we are going to tackle the face recognition problem.

Summary

In this chapter we learned what the convolutional network layers are learning. Then we went through topics such as neural style transfer, minimizing the cost function, and so on. We also saw how to build a neural network that produces art.

Face Recognition 6

In this chapter, we will explore the challenges and the solutions related to the face recognition problem. Therefore, we are going to first present the face recognition problem nature and the similarity function as the general high-level solution. Then, we will introduce Siamese networks, which, together with the similarity function, constitute the fundamental techniques for solving face detection in an efficient manner. From there, we will proceed with two ways that have shown excellent results in training the convolutional neural network for face detection; the triplet loss function and binary classification. Finally, we will see how to use inception network like GoogLeNet and similar transfer learning and the triplet cost function to build the Java face recognition application. Additionally, we will be going through the code details and building a Java application.

The following are the topics that we will be covering in this chapter:

- Problems in face detection
- Differentiating inputs with Siamese networks
- Exploring triplet loss
- Binary classification
- Building face recognition application

 The code will be published on GitHub and it will continually be updated to offer better performance in the future: https://github.com/ PacktPublishing/Hands-On-Java-Machine-Learning-for-Computer- Vision

Problems in face detection

Let's explore these challenges related to face recognition:

- Face versification versus face recognition
- One-shot learning

We will also see a high-level solution to these problems.

Face verification versus face recognition

So far, we have seen the image recognition problem, where the model predicted either image at any of the chosen classes or objects, such as is it a car, or perhaps a pedestrian, and so on. In addition to that, we have also seen the object localization and detection, where we put a bounding box to those classes or chosen objects. But for now, that is not important. Anyway, in both the cases, we are interested in establishing whether an image had a certain type of object.

Face verification

Now, we are going one step further by uniquely identifying the object itself, so not just the type, but we are interested in the unique object:

So we will not just identify whether the image is a car or not, but rather, will also find out if it is specifically my car, your car, or someone's else's car. And for animal detection, we may identify someone's cat or dog, not just if the image has a general dog entry. This is the object verification problem; face verification is not different, merely the logic is extended to the human face, and it may be a bit more sensitive, since identifying the wrong person can have a lot of consequences, but the logic stays the same.

The question here is not simply whether the object in the image is a human or pedestrian, but rather whether it is a person with **ID X**, or perhaps a company employee with some specific number:

Face recognition

Then we have the face recognition problem, where we need to perform face verification, but rather for a group of people.

In other words identifying whether there is a known person in a group of people:

Although face recognition and verification can be thought as the same problem, the reason we treat them as different is because the face recognition is much harder.

For instance, if we achieve the face verification of **98%** accuracy, if a person is the one that it claims, it may be not that bad, so maybe this accuracy could be, in some cases, acceptable. Now, if we apply that model with **2%** error rate to the face recognition, with **16** people in this instance, then we have a **32%** error rate, since we have **2%** for each of these photos:

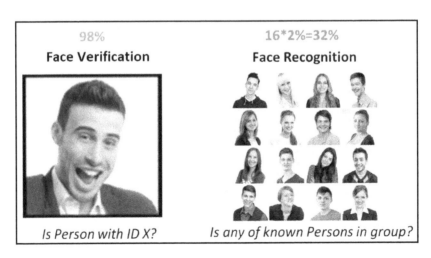

And obviously, it is not going to work well, since this level of error is quite significant. So, for face recognition to work well and have a reasonable level of accuracy, also taking into account the sensitive information of the topic, we'll need something like 99.999% accuracy.

One-shot learning problem

The second challenge is related to one-shot learning problem. Usually with face recognition, we have only one photo of each of the persons to recognize. So let's say that we want to recognize employees as they arrive in the morning.

Usually, you really could have just one photo of the employee, or maybe in the best cases, very few of them.

With the knowledge we now have, we can, of course, feed all these photos to a convolution neural network, and through a softmax, could have the number of classes as a number of employees:

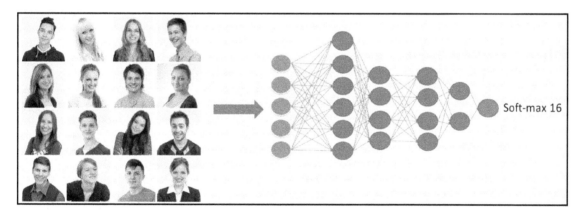

Actually, that will not work well, and we could not have really robust prediction. Convolution architecture has so far demonstrated really promising results, but don't forget that training involved thousands of images of one type, and two million images in total. Additionally, this solution will not scale as well.

So, this is what will happen if we have a new employee:

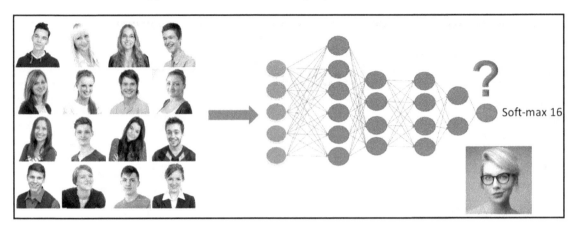

We need to modify the softmax to have 70 outputs. So does that mean that we need to retrain the neural network each time an employee comes in?

Similarity function

The high-level solution to the problems is through the similarity function, which states the following:

- $d(face\_1, face\_2)$: Degree of difference between images
- $d(face\_1, face\_2) < \gamma$: Means same face else, not same

This means, instead of trying to learn to recognize a specific person's face, what if we learn a function, d, which measures how similar or different two images are. If the function were to return a value smaller than a constant, such as gamma, then we say this is the same face or the same image. Otherwise, we say, they are different.

Suppose on the left we have the employee's faces, and on the right there is a person coming in:

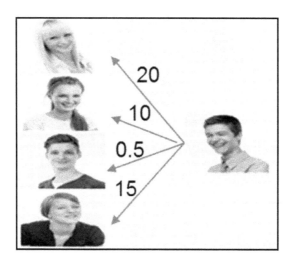

We will have numbers returned by the *d* function, and in the first two cases, we see that we have big numbers, because actually these two images, and these two people are different. Well, the third case had a really small number, and if we have a constant such as 0.8 or something, then, we have the function output that these images are the same. And for the fourth case, naturally we have a high number.

Additionally, this solution also scales well, since if a new person is joining, that would mean just a new comparison to execute. We don't have any new neural network to train or such thing because the *d* function is quite general. We are learning a function to measure how similar two images are, rather than learning a specific face.

Let's now move on to searching solutions for face recognition.

Differentiating inputs with Siamese networks

Let's see how the similarity function is implemented through Siamese networks. The idea was first implemented at paper published by Taigman in 2014, *DeepFace: Closing the Gap to Human-Level Performance in Face Verification*. Then we will see how Siamese networks learn by giving a slightly more formal definition.

First, we will continue to use convolution architectures with many convolution layers:

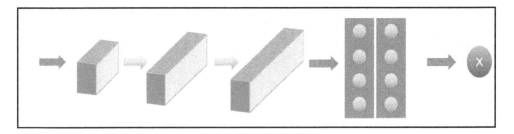

The fully connected layers within neurons, and the softmax for the prediction.

Let's fit the first image we want to compare, $\mathbf{X^1}$:

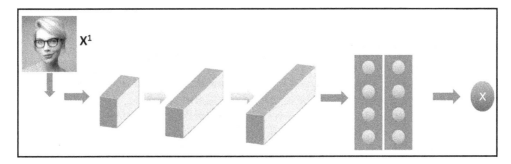

And what we will do is, through a forward pass, grab the activation values of the last fully connected layer, and we will refer to those values as $\mathbf{F(x^1)}$, or sometimes also the encoded values of the image, because we transform this image through the forward paths to another set of values of the activation of the last fully connected layer:

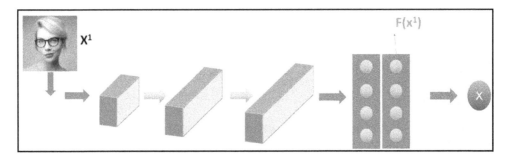

And that will be saved in the memory. We will repeat the same for the second image we want to compare, in other words, X^2:

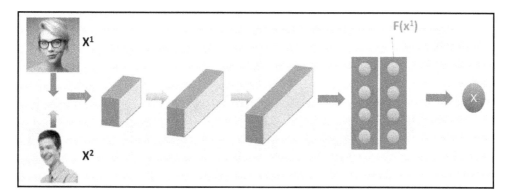

We'll do a forward pass, and then we will gain the $F(x^2)$, which refers to the encoded values for the second image:

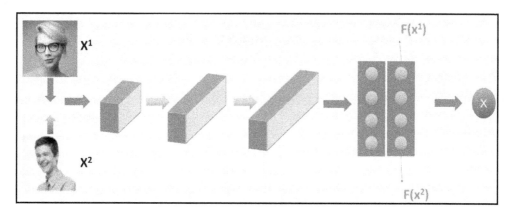

Notice that the network here stays the same for both of the images. And that's where this Siamese name comes in; since we are using the same network execution for both of the images, in practice, these forward passes are happening in parallel.

By now, it is clear that the softmax layer is redundant, so we didn't use it at all. So let's remove it, and instead, replace with the difference of the encoded values between the two images:

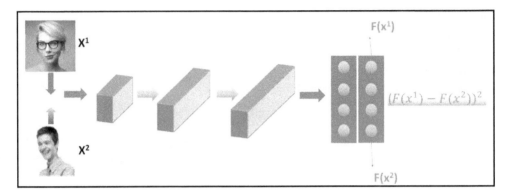

And only when the accounted values are similar, which means that this difference is close to zero, we'll predict that the two images are the same. Otherwise, if the difference between the encoded values is large, this means that these images are different as well. Since, by means of the forward pass, we gain a transformation of the image, which simply describes the image itself, so if those encoded values are different, that indirectly means that the images are different as well.

As you will recall from the previous section, this is exactly what we referred to as similarity function d:

$$d = (F(x^1) - F(x^2))$$

The d denotes the distance between the encoded activation of the last layer of some deep convolution network, such as an inception network. Since this is just a comparison, a question may arise: why don't we compare the image pixels instead of using a forward pass to gain the activation values of the last layer? The reason that would not work well is because, even a slight change on image light will make the pixel distance too big, while the encoded values offer a more robust representation of the image, since the neural network already learned the tricks to observe those differences through intensive training and a lot of data.

Learning with Siamese networks

Let's see now how Siamese network will learn to detect if two images are the same or not. First, we will fit as we solve both of the images:

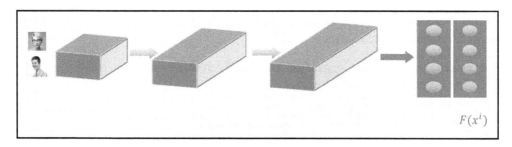

And, in the end, we will gain the activation values in the last layer, and store those in memory of course.

Next, the derivation is calculated, and the feedback from that derivation will be back propagated to change the network weights in such a way that if the images are similar, then the difference of the encoded values will be small, while if the images are different, then the back propagation step will change the weights in such a way that will cause the difference of the activation values of the last layer or the encoded values to be large:

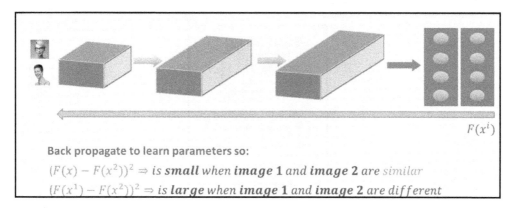

In a few words, this will be our goal of learning to ship the difference accordingly to small or large number depending if the images are the same or different.

Exploring triplet loss

In this section, we shall look at the finer details of the cost function with a triplet loss. We will train network weights using the triplet cost function or the triplet loss. The idea was introduced in the paper by Schroff in 2015, *FaceNet: A unified embedding for face recognition and clustering*. We shall also explore the areas to choose the triplet so that our network will learn to achieve really high accuracy.

We begin by choosing the base or anchor image, which will be used as a sample for other comparts. The base image is as follows:

Anchor

We shall now select a different image that represents the same person; this is known as the positive image, shown as follows:

Positive

AS we have seen in the previous section, we want the similarity function *d* as close to zero as possible. It is mathematically expressed as:

$$d(A,P) = (F(A) - F(P))^2 \approx 0$$

Having this value close to zero means that the encoded values for the anchor image and positive image will be almost the same. This also implies that the images are the same, which is exactly what we want, in this case.

To understand this better, let's keep the anchor image constant, and change the positive image to that of a different person, which would be known as a negative image:

Negative

Here the distance function or the similarity function will produce a much larger value:

$$d(A,N) = (F(A) - F(N))^2 > 0$$

The reason we want a big value here is because we want the encoded values of the anchor image and the native image to be different, which implies that the images are different. This would help the neural network figure out the difference in the two.

The name triplet is a derivative of the fact that we now require three images: the anchor image, the positive image, and the negative image, as compared to the classical case where we use two images. To understand this better, for one sample, let's use three images and feed this to a convolution architecture, but before we jump into this, let's take a look at the definition of triplet loss:

$$(F(A) - F(P))^2 \approx 0 \; ; \; (F(A) - F(N))^2 > 0$$

We have the two similarity functions, the positive similarity function and the negative similarity function. The negative similarity function tends to be greater than zero, while the positive similarity function tends to go to zero.

If we replace the zero with the functions, will have the following equation:

$$(F(A) - F(P))^2 \leq (F(A) - F(N))^2$$

So, the similarity function of a positive case will have to be smaller than the similarity function of the negative case. This makes perfect sense, since we want the distance between the images of the same person to be considerably smaller than the distance between the images of different people.

Let's solve this equation mathematically:

$$(F(A) - F(P))^2 - (F(A) - F(N))^2 \leq 0$$

This holds mathematically true, and we have an equation that satisfies our conditions.

In practice, a neural network could cheat by finding out the weights, so that the distances will have the same value. The neural network usually figures out weights in a few iterations, which causes the distance of the positive case to be the same as the distance of the negative case. And if they are the same, then our equation will be equal to zero. In this situation, even though our condition is satisfied, the network really learns nothing.

To solve this, we shall add a constant $-\epsilon$ value as follows:

$$(F(A) - F(P))^2 - (F(A) - F(N))^2 \leq -\varepsilon$$

The neural network has to work harder to produce at least a minimum difference of $-\epsilon$ between the two similar functions. If the condition is not satisfied, the neural network will have to keep trying for any number of iterations. Solving this equation further, we get the following:

$$(F(A) - F(P))^2 - (F(A) - F(N))^2 + \varepsilon \leq 0$$

Let us assume that the positive case produces an output of 0.5 and the ϵ value is equal to 0.2:

$$0.5 - (F(A) - F(N))^2 + 0.2 \leq 0$$

The neural network will try to learn the weights that would help us attain some distance function for the negative image. Let's assume that it tries to cheat the equation the first time, by having 0.5, which is the same value as the positive image distance. The equation will not be satisfied as the final answer will be greater than zero, which is the exact opposite of what we require.

The following occasion, it assumes the negative distance value to be 0.7. This perfectly satisfies the condition.

For the next iteration, we can chose values 0.5, 0.3, and such until the final value obtained is less than 0.

This step-by-step, iteration-by-iteration approach helps us increase the negative cost function up as we want the difference of different values to be a greater value and decrease the positive cost function to reduce the difference.

Choosing the triplets

Choosing the triplets is very important as it impacts the learning of the network.

For negative cases, we just choose them randomly, and most of the time, they actually satisfy the equation easily. The reason for this is, the difference between the anchor and negative image is already great. Thus, no matter the value that you choose, the difference will always be large. We can express this mathematically as the following:

> When negative examples N are chosen randomly then the condition is easily satisfied: d(A,P)+"ε"≤"d(A,N)"; since d(A,N) will be always big enough

The network at this point will get lazy and not solve the equations for the upcoming iterations. To resolve this, we need to choose triplets that are complex to train:

> Choose triplets that are hard to train d(A,P)+"ε"≤"d(A,N)"; so network has to push up hard d(A,N) and down d(A,P) to satisfy the margin "ε"

This means that we need to choose a negative case that is as similar as the anchor network; this will lead to smaller distance values, thus making the neural network work hard to attain the requisite results.

The same applies to the positive case, where we use an image that is not very similar to the anchor image, making the neural network work for a greater number of iterations to achieve the desired result.

During the training process, we need several positive example images. Assume we have 100 employees for the system we already mentioned in the previous section, we may need more than 1,000 images. This gives us an average of 10 positive images per person.

While testing, we may apply the famous one-shot learning, so if a new employee comes in, we don't need to retrain anything because we have a general way to encode the images that we keep in the database. If a new person joins the company, we basically just encode the face image, and we compare it to the one in the database.

This resolves the one-shot learning and the scaling is automatically solved, but again, during the training, we may need several positive examples.

Binary classification

In this section, we will begin by looking at the formal definition of the triplet loss function and how to choose the triplets.

We'll continue to use CMS networks, which will help us gain the encoded values for the last fully connected layers.

In the following two diagrams, notice that the comparison made here is the triplet loss. Labelled data is made up of two images instead of three:

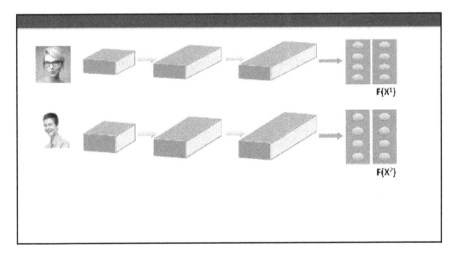

In this case, instead of using the similarity function, we shall use binary classification. When it comes to binary classification, we use the logistic regression unit:

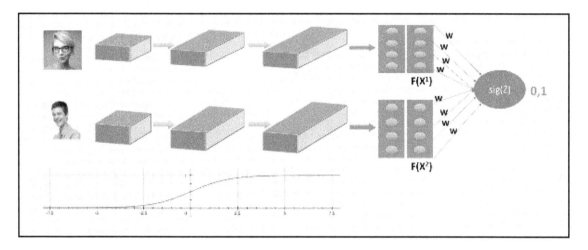

So we will feed each of these units, multiply them by the weights, sum up these values, and give to the sigmoid function that will give us an output of one for a positive value and zero for a negative image. Here, we shall use it in a similar manner, where zero would indicate that the images are different and one would indicate that the images are the same.

Post this, using various forward and back propagation steps, we train our neural network to predict the data.

Let's consider a case where the images are different. We start with the forward pass that we feed to the logistics unit and obtain a prediction. Now, we carry out back propagation and change the weight to optimize the network to obtain an output close to zero.

Binary classification cost function

Let's look at a detailed view of the logistic unit and the cost function. We are going to use the logistic unit in a different manner. Before feeding our data directly to the logistic unit, we will first calculate the difference between each of these units, and only then will we multiply this difference by the weight, and then fit it to the logistic unit. This can be expressed mathematically expressed as follows:

$$Z = sum(W_k * (f(X_i^1) - f(X_i^2)) + b)$$
$$Y = sig(Z); 0|1$$

We take the difference of each of these units and then multiply it with some weights. Sum up all the values and apply it to the sigmoid function that could output zero and one.

We could complicate this formula by writing it in this form:

$$Z = sum(W_k * \frac{(f(X_i^1) - f(X_i^2))^2}{f(X_i^1) + f(X_i^2)} + b)$$

Here, we calculate the squared difference and then divide it by the sum. We then, sum up these values and apply it to a sigmoid function.

We could keep on complicating this formula, but the ideology stays the same.

Building a face recognition Java application

We are going through the code details of building a Java face recognition application, and by the end of this section, we shall be able to create a live demo version of the recognition application.

Let's begin with exploring the code by creating a basic network:

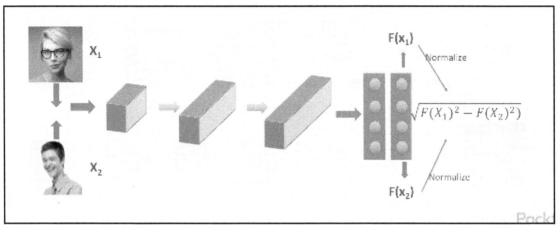

Training the model for face recognition is time consuming and hard. To take care of this, we shall be using transfer recognition and to obtain pre-trained weights. The time model we choose is based on the inception network GoogLeNet, and this will be used to obtain the encodings or the activations of the last layer. Post this, instead of calculating the distance between them directly, we shall normalize the encodings using the L2-norm and only after this, we shall use the distance between the images.

Notice that we are not using the squared distance but rather just the Euclidean distance between the images, which is different from what we have seen previously.

Usually, we have a certain number of people. For the same of this example, let us consider this as the number of employees:

If we want to gauge if the person who is entering the premises is someone new or an employee. For each of the employees, we are going to calculate the encoding, and save them in our database, or in memory. These images will be fed to the pre-trained model, which will give us the activation function defined in the previous diagram. More specifically, we are going to save the database with a normalized version of these activation functions.

In case there is a new person, we need to check if the picture lies in the database. We start with calculating the normalized activation values of the last layer for this new photo:

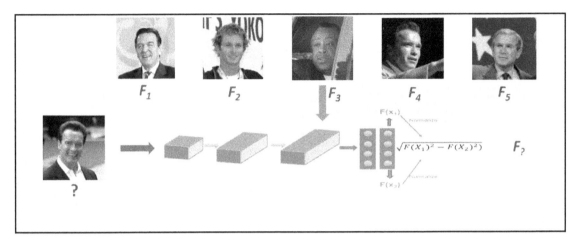

The new person is labelled as a question mark. Moving ahead, we calculate the distance of this image with all the images in the database.

Among all of these, we shall choose the image that has the least distance from the new image. We can set a threshold of 0.5 or 0.6 beyond, which will classify the person as unknown:

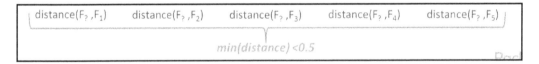

Here, hopefully the minimum distance is between our new image and image four should stay below the 0.5 threshold, implying that this new person is actually someone from our database.

Let's look at the code to do this:

```
public class FaceNetSmallV2Model {
private int numClasses = 0;
 private final long seed = 1234;
 private int[] inputShape = new int[]{3, 96, 96};
 private IUpdater updater = new Adam(0.1, 0.9, 0.999, 0.01);
 private int encodings = 128;
 public static int reluIndex = 1;
 public static int paddingIndex = 1;
public ComputationGraphConfiguration conf() {
```

```
computationGraphConfiguration.GraphBuilder graph = new
NeuralNetConfiguration.Builder().seed(seed)
 .activation(Activation.IDENTITY)
 .optimizationAlgo(OptimizationAlgorithm.STOCHASTIC_GRADIENT_DESCENT)
 .updater(updater)
 .weightInit(WeightInit.RELU)
 .l2(5e-5)
 .miniBatch(true)
 .graphBuilder();
```

First we have the model. As we mentioned this is a model quite similar to the inception network, but of course a bit smaller than it, although the code looks a bit large, it adds this layer according to the open source implementation in Keras of this GitHub project:

```
buildBlock3a(graph);
buildBlock3b(graph);
buildBlock3c(graph);

buildBlock4a(graph);
buildBlock4e(graph);

buildBlock5a(graph);
buildBlock5b(graph);
```

So first layers are quite manual till these three bs or we can add them here. We merge all of these together, and then append this block to the previous block and so on. But then, block for ae and so on are a bit more automated; we use this utility method here to append these blocks more easily.

At the end of the code, we have the final layers, which is this dense layer, fully connected neurons. We are going to use 128 of such neurons, because this has proven to give good results, and as we already mentioned, instead of using those activations directly, we are going to use the *l2* normalization version of them, which is why we add the vertex here, *l2* normalization vertex.

Usually, loading the weights with the Deepleaning4j is quite easy. This time it is different, because the weight we have our speed up in some axles. The way we are going to load these weights is like with this method here:

```
  static void loadWeights(ComputationGraph computationGraph) throws
  IOException
  {

          Layer[] layers = computationGraph.getLayers();
          for (Layer layer : layers) {
              List<double[]> all = new ArrayList<>();
              String layerName = layer.conf().getLayer().getLayerName();
```

```
            if (layerName.contains("bn")) {
                all.add(readWightsValues(BASE + layerName + "_w.csv"));
                all.add(readWightsValues(BASE + layerName + "_b.csv"));
                all.add(readWightsValues(BASE + layerName + "_m.csv"));
                all.add(readWightsValues(BASE + layerName + "_v.csv"));
                layer.setParams(mergeAll(all));
            } else if (layerName.contains("conv")) {
                all.add(readWightsValues(BASE + layerName + "_b.csv"));
                all.add(readWightsValues(BASE + layerName + "_w.csv"));
                layer.setParams(mergeAll(all));
            } else if (layerName.contains("dense")) {
                double[] w = readWightsValues(BASE + layerName + "_w.csv");
                all.add(w);
                double[] b = readWightsValues(BASE + layerName + "_b.csv");
                all.add(b);
                layer.setParams(mergeAll(all));
            }
        }
    }
```

We build up the model to have similar layer names with those files, and then we locate the layer name. Based on the layer name we are going to find those axles, merge them together, and set as the layer parameters.

Notice from the convolution at dense there is a slight difference. In Deeplearning4j the convolution expressed bias first, while even though we have the dense layer, we have the weight first. So, switching this will actually cause the model to not work properly.

Then we have the prediction phase, where we define what the method is. The code is as follows:

```
    public String whoIs(String imagePath) throws IOException {
        INDArray read = read(imagePath);
        INDArray encodings = forwardPass(normalize(read));
        double minDistance = Double.MAX_VALUE;
        String foundUser = "";
        for (Map.Entry<String, INDArray> entry :
    memberEncodingsMap.entrySet()) {
            INDArray value = entry.getValue();
            double distance = distance(value, encodings);
            log.info("distance of " + entry.getKey() + " with " + new
    File(imagePath).getName() + " is " + distance);
            if (distance < minDistance) {
                minDistance = distance;
                foundUser = entry.getKey();
            }
        }
```

This will iterate through the map, which is what we have done in database or memory. We then need to get the encodings and calculate the distance between them.

This is the *l2* distance. If the distance is smaller than the minimum, we register the user. But remember this is not the end, we are also going to do this final check, so if minimum distance is greater than the threshold, the user is an unknown user:

```
if (minDistance > THRESHOLD) {
        foundUser = "Unknown user";
    }
    log.info(foundUser + " with distance " + minDistance);
    return foundUser;
```

Only when the minimum distance is smaller than threshold, only then we know that this person exists in database. Let's now see what the application will look like. Here, we have the images that exist in in our database, and at the top left, we can load the images and compare them against what we have:

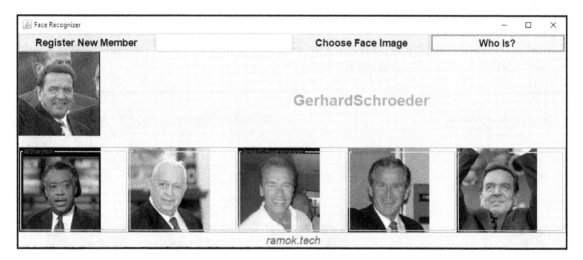

For example, here we load this person, which is **GerhardSchroeder**, and it actually matches one of the images in our database.

Let's choose another one, such as Arnold Schwarzenegger we saw previously, so it was able to actually detect this image in here. Now, let's choose another one as follows:

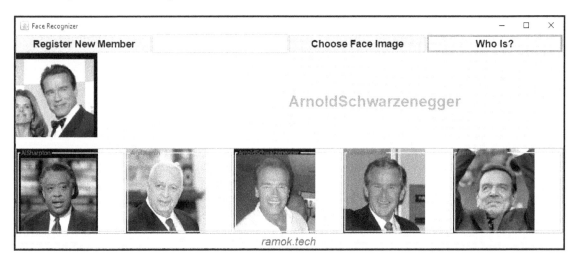

Actually, the application offers a feature for registering new persons. We could select a new person, and click on the **Register New Member** button:

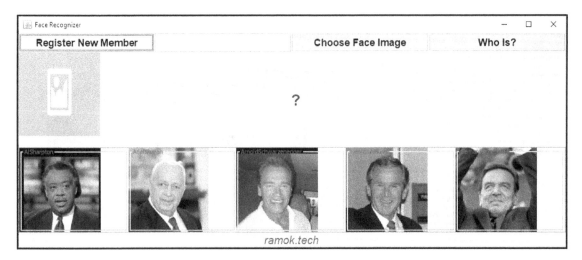

The application could be tuned and trained further. So it has some room for improvement, especially with the way it consolidates the data, as we have not applied the standard approach.

Summary

In this chapter, we have explored the challenges faced when building a face recognition application. Post this, the solution to these problems was bought to light, and we worked our way through the multiple possibilities in terms of dealing with the challenges.

Other Books You May Enjoy

If you enjoyed this book, you may be interested in these other books by Packt:

Practical Computer Vision
Abhinav Dadhich

ISBN: 978-1-78829-768-4

- Learn the basics of image manipulation with OpenCV
- Implement and visualize image filters such as smoothing, dilation, histogram equalization, and more
- Set up various libraries and platforms, such as OpenCV, Keras, and Tensorflow, in order to start using computer vision, along with appropriate datasets for each chapter, such as
- MSCOCO, MOT, and Fashion-MNIST
- Understand image transformation and downsampling with practical implementations.
- Explore neural networks for computer vision and convolutional neural networks using Keras

Deep Learning for Computer Vision
Rajalingappaa Shanmugamani

ISBN: 978-1-78829-562-8

- Set up an environment for deep learning with Python, Tensorflow, and Keras
- Define and train a model for image and video classification
- Use features from a pre-trained Convolutional Neural Network model for image retrieval
- Understand and implement object detection using the real-world Pedestrian Detection scenario
- Learn about various problems in image captioning and how to overcome them by training images and text together

Leave a review - let other readers know what you think

Please share your thoughts on this book with others by leaving a review on the site that you bought it from. If you purchased the book from Amazon, please leave us an honest review on this book's Amazon page. This is vital so that other potential readers can see and use your unbiased opinion to make purchasing decisions, we can understand what our customers think about our products, and our authors can see your feedback on the title that they have worked with Packt to create. It will only take a few minutes of your time, but is valuable to other potential customers, our authors, and Packt. Thank you!

Index

www.ingramcontent.com/pod-product-compliance
Lightning Source LLC
Chambersburg PA
CBHW080635060326
40690CB00021B/4935